Being Successful in... Buc

About the Author

Evelyn Hempenstall is a chartered accountant operating as a senior financial controller with significant commercial expertise in the areas of operational and financial planning and management in performance-led organisations.

Being Successful in...

Budgeting

Evelyn Hempenstall

BLACKHALL
Publishing

This book was typeset by
Artwerk
for
Blackhall Publishing
26 Eustace Street
Dublin 2
Ireland

e-mail: blackhall@tinet.ie

ISBN: 1 901657 27 2

A catalogue record for this book is available from the British Library.

Printed in Ireland by
Betaprint Ltd

Series Foreword

*The Being Successful in...*series is a new series of practical books, which provide an accessible and user friendly approach to the common problems experienced by small to medium-sized, growing businesses.

The series will help businesses in the start-up phase but also covers problems encountered during the all-important development phase. They will be helpful to businesses which are starting to grow and which need to cope with a range of unfamiliar, difficult and often competing issues.

The books in the series are comprehensive and yet concise, and they treat the topics in question succinctly and without recourse to jargon. Practical examples, checklists and pointers on to further sources of help and advice are included to supplement the text.

Books published in the *Being Successful in..*series in early 1999:
Being Successful in...Report Writing
Being Successful in...Customer Care
Being Successful in...Presentations
Being Successful in...Time Management
Being Successful in...Patents, Copyright & Trade Marks

Forthcoming books in the series:
Being Successful in...Overcoming Stress
Being Successful in...Winning Business
Being Successful in...Business Planning
Being Successful in...Public Relations

I hope you find this book useful.
Veronica Canning
October 1998

Contents

To Claire Hempenstall, of course

Chapter 1

Why Budgeting Is Vital

This chapter will help you to:

- understand what the processes and techniques of budgeting can do for your business;

- see that there is more to budgeting than merely cost control;

- determine the most appropriate budget structure and budget period for your business.

Why Budgeting Is Vital

WHAT IS A BUDGET?

A budget is a plan for the future activities of an organisation. It can be expressed in a number of ways but mainly it is expressed in financial terms simply because it is in financial terms that all aspects of the business can be described. Many non-financial or quantitative measures can, and indeed should, also be incorporated into your plan to make it relevant to your business.

A budget is the standard device by which any business can seriously assess its present standing in a changing environment and prepare a strategic plan to close the gap between desired and likely results.

WHY IS BUDGETING OF USE TO YOU?

Budgeting is recommended as an important technique that helps management in at least six ways!

1. By forcing managers to **plan** ahead and reduce the number of ad hoc decisions.

2. By aiding **communication** as those in top management set out objectives and other members of the business team indicate the problems and opportunities they see ahead.

3. By aiding **co-ordination** as separate functional departments provide their individual inputs which have to be merged and reconciled during the budget process.

4. By setting out clearly defined targets which, if set at the appropriate level of difficulty and accepted by managers, aid **motivation**.

5. By providing standards and plans which can be employed as part of the **control** process.

6. By providing a yardstick against which managers and their individual and department performance can be evaluated – **performance monitoring**.

A Plan

The production of the plan or budget is of itself an excellent exercise for any business. The initial stages of compiling budgets encourage individuals, departments and the business itself to look ahead and plan – taking account of all the circumstances, calculating likely revenues, working out probable expenditure, being aware of possible influences on them and so forth.

Clearly, both the preliminary and ongoing planning, which is required as revised and new budgets are drawn up and agreed, is advantageous. This is because it helps to identify the viability of different activities, their likely consequences, cash flow effect and probable profits and losses well in advance. Thus you can act *before* rather than *after* to take advantage of opportunities and to avoid problems.

> **WORD TO THE WISE**
> There are a number of significant ways that budgeting can help management in achieving its business goals. The benefits of good budgeting will always exceed the cost.

A Co-ordinator

Preparing the components that make up the total budget of the business and then bringing them together, is a very effective tool to help co-ordinate the activities and priorities of employees and departments within a firm.

The objective should be that everyone knows his or her own budget inside out, agrees with it and understands how it fits in with the other departments or responsibilities, so recognising the knock-on effect that will occur if budgets are surpassed or not achieved.

Budgeting can be a unifying influence with everyone working as part of a team to make sure that they all succeed by achieving the maximum revenues and not exceeding the targeted costs.

The key to this level of co-ordination is an understanding by individuals or departments of their role within the total scheme of things and the setting of common, well-understood goals, which override sectional interests. Ultimately the management must define these goals and set out the criteria by which issues, such as scarce resources, timing and how each discipline can effect the total business process, will be resolved.

A Motivator

The process of budgeting and continuously apraised performance can motivate people to work harder and do better. In essence budgets establish the required standards and, consequently, become goals that need to be reached. These goals include attaining specified revenues by certain dates, maintaining a positive cash flow or planning for funding requirements to keep expenditure within agreed limits, etc.

While it is, of course, obvious that employees are motivated in innumerable ways there is a substantial recognition that the chance to achieve challenging targets, to be recognised as successful, and be praised and rewarded is a powerful incentive.

Control

Budgets are an important part of an effective management information system and show the financial implications of business plans and policies. If budgets are related to the responsibilities of those that actually generate revenues or costs and are compared to actual results, then budgets are part of the management control system and the business is using budgetary control.

The later stages of trying to adhere to budgets (and hopefully succeeding) enable individuals, departments and the business generally to exercise a considerable degree of control over their activities. This is done by comparing estimated and actual results, identifying variances and, most importantly, by taking the corrective action needed either to remedy problems or take advantage of opportunities.

Taking action is both the key to effective budgetary control and the ultimate indicator of effective management. Using budgeting as a control is also a very effective way to ensure that your business has the information and structures in place to take action before difficulties are insurmountable.

Performance Measurement

A key element in budgeting is the feedback of information comparing actual revenue and expenditure to budget projections. Performance monitoring shows who is responsible for each element in the budget and gives a sound basis for deciding what actions are necessary to improve the achievement of objectives. In many respects, budgeting could be said to create a framework for individuals, departments and the business as a whole to work within and defines the goals to work towards.

Budgeting sets out the financial and operational responsibilities of supervisors and managers, making them answerable for the successes and failures of their sections and departments. Everyone understands precisely what they and their teams have to achieve to stay on course. It also quantifies the overall financial and operational objectives of the business, towards which everyone should be working.

NON-FINANCIAL PERFORMANCE MEASUREMENT

The use of appropriate non-financial performance measurements is becoming a recognised part of the ideal budget management structure. These can be used to enhance the measurement of the achievement of the business goals, which are critical to long-term survival and success. The best approach to establishing what non-financial performance measure are appropriate to your business is to consider a range of possible measures under the following critical headings.

- **Having a customer perspective.**

  All business exists to satisfy customer requirements. In order to compete successfully, there is a need to focus on the customer and to measure performance against customer-driven criteria, e.g. on-time delivery performance, complete and accurate shipments and error-free transactions.

  The question is: How do customers see us?

- **The internal and business perspective.**

  Building capability internally is essential to becoming, and remaining, competitive. If you are a service company dependent on the skill mix of your employees, e.g. in the software development industry or in the telesales industry, your process capacity is determined by your training and recruitment policies. If you don't have a skill to sell you are out of business.

The question is: What must we excel at?

- **The innovation and learning perspective.**

Modern competitiveness is based on fulfilling customer requirements through creativity and innovation. The textile manufacturer who does not keep at the leading-edge of product design and so doesn't develop washable and easy-care fabrics for the clothing market will not remain competitive in the sports clothing market.

The question is: Can we continue to improve and create value?

- **The financial perspective focusing on the return the owners of the business receive.**

The shareholders or financial backets of your business are also a type of customer and adding value to these people has to be continuously monitored and measured. The standard budget targets will have the financial perspective built into the figures and tools such as financial ratios and key performance indicators will be useful in this regard.

The question is: How do we look to the owners or financial backers?

SHOULD ALL BUSINESS SET A BUDGET?

The advantages which budgets offer, provide an apparently overwhelming case for employing them in all types and sizes of business and at all stages of development. Despite difficulties with some dysfunctional behavioural consequences which budgets tend to generate, most companies do set budgets.

Budgetary systems are more common in larger companies, where formalised and sophisticated techniques are developed to serve the management. However, the usefulness of budgeting to small concerns cannot be understated. The death (and unwarranted creation) of many small businesses could have been avoided by an early attempt to quantify the dreams of headstrong but sloppy-thinking entrepreneurs who never directly faced the uncertainties of their venture.

A small business moved in to a lush market for medical equipment with high hopes. However, failure to quantify the long collection periods, to forecast a maximum sales potential and to control cost from the outset resulted in disaster within a year. Budgets for small business need not be as elaborate as those outlined in many more technical texts, but some level of good budgeting is imperative to an enterprise of any size.

HOW TO COPE WITH UNCERTAINTY

Many will claim that the uncertainties peculiar to their business make budgets impractical for them. Yet one can always find at least some companies in the same industry that use budgets successfully. Such companies are usually among the industry leaders and they regard budgets as indispensable aids. The point is that managers must grapple with uncertainties, either with a budget or without one. The benefits of good budgeting will always exceed its cost.

In a particularly fast changing environment or a start up situation, the way to cope with uncertainty is to accept that you may need to set shorter budget periods or to use flexible budgeting techniques to cope with your businesses individual circumstances. The golden rule should be that budgeting is an accepted practice no matter what the business environment throws at you but it is up to you to use budgeting techniques and procedures that are relevant and useful.

WHAT WILL YOU USE YOUR BUDGET FOR?

In a well-run business the budget can be used for any or all of the following:

- allocate resources;
- quantify plans;
- co-ordinate departmental activities;
- communicate management plans and objectives;
- motivate;
- plan and control business performance;
- set end-performance goals for incentives;
- set performance objectives and targets.

In order that your budgeting serves this range of purposes you are going to require some form of structure both to start and to run the process. Keep in mind that your business priorities will be changing constantly and you will need to adapt your budgeting process to serve your changing needs.

BUDGETING STRUCTURE

The general structure of your budgets must reflect the organisation and responsibility levels within your company. Despite underlying similarities, no two organisations, and therefore no two master budgets, are identical.

There are however, factors which are generally common to all budgets.

- Business, financial and operating objectives.
- Organisational structure and personnel policies.
- Product and service strategy.
- Production, distribution, selling and administrative functions.
- Market identification and marketing methods.
- Capital investment requirements.
- Direct resources consumed and direct costs.
- Pricing policy and pricing structure.
- Sales and service delivery.
- Overhead costs.
- Revenues.
- Key financial statements, which will include as a minimum the profit and loss statement, balance sheet and cash or funds flow statement.

BUDGET PERIOD

The time span for which budgets are commonly prepared is one year, but it may be longer or shorter. In deciding what is appropriate to your business you should consider some of the following issues.

1. The budget period affects both the form and content of the plan

For example:
- short-term budgets of one year or less emphasise short-term control and operating profitability;

- medium-term budgets of one to three years emphasise the filling of gaps in current business strengths the balance between capital and current spending and provide the marker for required change;
- long-term budgets of three years or more emphasise the development of viable business strategies which will secure long-term survival.

2. You should consider what the natural business year or cycle is for your business

A majority of businesses use the calender year as their budget period. This can be useful particularly for motivational purposes – starting the new year afresh, etc. However, it is important to consider the best dates on which the budget period should start and end. Most service or product-oriented companies have a definite cycle of activities covering one year and there may be one or more periods when sales and activity peak.

Since the activities being co-ordinated by the budget, such as producing in anticipation of selling, often fall into different months, it is vital to make sure they do not also fall into different budget periods. Otherwise the benefits of budgeting in planning and co-ordinating your business may be lost.

A clothing manufacturer of fashion garments has two peak selling periods in the year (to service the spring and winter seasons) and each of these seasons has a production and distribution cycle. There is little use in setting a budget period that does not encompass all three parts of the cycle in one time period.

3. Seasonal factors

Many factors important to your business can be subject to seasonal variation. These should be identified, incorporated into the preparation of the budget and, later, in reporting performance. The retail jewellery business, for example, will plan a significant part of its work of purchasing, investment in stock, promotion and selling around the Christmas and St Valentine's Day gift markets.

4. Appropriate control period

While short-term budgets normally apply to a one-year period you may require your budget to apply for shorter intervals for control purposes, so that action can be taken if actual results do not match the budget targets.

5. Projects/Long-term contracts

It makes little sense for a business whose activity is generated through project activity, whether long or short-term, to deal only with a traditional year budget period when the process of assigning the timing of profitability during the life of a project can very often be nothing more than an accounting exercise.

The appropriate budget programme for such a business would set a planning and reporting structure for each project and annual budgets would be primarily focused on top level issues, such as balance sheet reporting.

PRIOR PREPARATION AND APPROVAL

Budgets should be prepared in advance of the time period for which they are to be used. Surprisingly this requirement often goes ignored. Some business managers would say that they have difficulty forecasting the next year's activity until the current year outcome is known. It would take either a poorly managed business or a very volatile environment to make it impossible to forecast, for example, the last remaining quarter of the current year.

Even in very changeable circumstances the budget can be prepared and agreed on the premise that it can be altered in the advent of changing short-term circumstances, such as the current year outcome.

IS CHANGING THE BUDGET A SIGN OF FAILURE?

No, not at all. Ideally all budgets should be flexible, with regular checks being made to them. Flexible budgets can allow for a re-evaluation of budget assumptions, limiting factors, external influences and it is useful that such amendments are incorporated in the budgets as and when they are appropriate.

A budget should not be rigid and unyielding with everything being categorised as a success or failure. The only failure would be to set an unrealistic budget and try to measure performance against it, come what may. Budgeting needs to be approached in a pragmatic manner in order to ensure that it is effective as a business tool and not an impediment to your success.

REMEMBER

DO:

- Consider the six ways in which budgeting can help your management of the business. By being aware of the various the uses of budgeting you can expand the use of the process to gain maximum benefit.

- Include in your budget the non-financial performance measures that will expand the use of your budget plan to all aspects of your business.

- Acknowledge that your business priorities will be constantly changing so you will need to adapt your budgeting process to suit your changing needs.

- Choose the best budget period for your business.

DO NOT:

- Assume that budgeting is not useful in a fast changing environment. Adapt the process by shortening the budget period or using flexible budgets.

Chapter 2

Budget Preparation: The Planning Process

This chapter will help you to:

- achieve your goal of developing a budgeting system that supports and enhances the success of your business;

- develop your business strategy;

- review your business with a budgeting eye;

- define your business objectives;

- set your financial and operating targets;

- learn what factors to consider in choosing the budget approach which best suits your business.

Budget Preparation: The Planning Process

INTRODUCTION

Your decision to embark on or improve your current budget preparation process must now be supported by a clear plan of action in order to arrive at your ultimate goal which is *to develop a budgeting system that actively supports the success of your business or department.*

Your present budgetary situation will dictate the starting point at which you attempt to improve or develop your budgeting process. If yourself are establishing a budget process for the first time for you or your business, you have an ideal opportunity to start and develop the process correctly for maximum effect. This initial stage is vital to your future success.

If you are a manager where the current budgeting process is already established you may feel that this chapter is not relevant to you. You have your budget preparation process in place, or imposed on you, and you are reasonably comfortable, but maybe not entirely happy with the value, effectiveness or timescale of the entire budget process. It is in these circumstances that a good, hard look at your business planning process will prove most useful indeed.

You will learn much that will allow you to question the usefulness of the process itself and could very well open the budget preparation out from just the annual number crunching exercise to a vital planning and management tool.

The following are your steps to success.
- Budgets must be based on a clear strategy.
- In order to determine the strategy you must review the business and compare it's present standing to the changing environment and prepare a strategic plan to close the gap between desired and likely results.
- This leads to the definition of business objectives.
- From these business objectives, your financial objectives and targets are developed and it is on these you will base your budgets.

Budgetary control must be based on the setting and achievement of sound financial objectives at all levels within your organisation. It is misleading to think in terms of a single objective.

STEP 1 : BUSINESS REVIEW PROCESS

The review process gives you and your team an opportunity to look at your business with an objective budgeting eye – it can be both an exhilarating and levelling process. The important thing is that it must be well informed and honest. This is not the time for fault-finding or fantasy – the lessons of the past should only be viewed as a tool to acting effectively in the future.

The popular SWOT analysis is a good starting point for the review process. It identifies:
- strengths;
- weaknesses;
- opportunities;
- threats.

A **strength** is any aspect of the organisation which is seen as being a current asset. They may be quality responsiveness, a commitment of staff, financial security, experience, etc.

A **weakness** is the opposite – either something that could be improved, such as poor reception facilities, or something that has to be lived with, such as poor road access.

An **opportunity** is something that could be taken advantage of in future – usually an external change that opens the door to do something new.

A **threat** is something that could happen, against which one might need to take defensive action – a review of the market, a potential loss of resources or goodwill for instance.

Your business premeses being in a bad state of repair is a weakness if it impairs capacity or confidence, but it could be a threat if your retail outlet is falling apart or if people stop coming to you because of it.

This type of review should be as multi-disciplinary as possible. It will almost certainly lead to identifying priorities, both short and long-term, to strengthen your position or exploit the opportunities open to your business.

I find the SWOT analysis particularly useful when combined with a check on the expectations of customers.

First identify all of them – both existing and targeted customers. This exercise can certainly be salutary. It is powerful to pose questions such as: "What do they want?" or "What do they say about us?" Remember the purpose of the review. You are trying to define your present status so that you can set your objectives for the future. Often information about attitudes and expectations is equally as important as hard activity and cost data.

In an existing business this service review may provide the starting point for developing the new business plan by reviewing the outcomes of the previous one.

STEP 2: BUSINESS STRATEGIC PLAN

The strategic plan will set out the major long-term goals for your business. This could simply be a matter of clearly stating what the definition of the business is and stating that you wish it to grow in terms of size, quality, competitiveness and security both for the benefit of the owners and the employees. It is from the definition of you strategic plan you will be able to set your all important business and financial objectives.

. It is important that you use a interactive business planning process with the members of your team to identify the goals of your business or department. Thus the term 'business planning' refers just as much to a developmental process as to a written plan. The creation of a written plan can become a valuable process in itself.

Team Planning

Creating the plan is an ideal way to open discussion about services which involves all the staff. There is no way for the manager to address expectations and secure the commitment of staff if the process of planning and review is not a team one. Quite often individual concerns and enthusiasms emerge from such team planning which give the manager valuable leads when it comes to defining objectives and developing plans.

The best way to start to develop a performance plan for a business or department is to set up business planning sessions, which are highly participatory and carefully planned to achieve this objective.

It is not difficult to develop appropriate team objectives from the priorities that emerge. If this is done annually, then it can be linked to the review of performance objectives and budget setting for the business. The process itself is both educational and unifying for all involved.

STEP 3: DECIDING BUSINESS OBJECTIVES

Business objectives consider the business as a whole and may be only partly quantifiable. Some objectives are quite general, others are more marketing, organisational or financial in nature. The business objectives need to be re-clarified from time to time and especially at the start of the budgeting process. The organisation changes, as does its environment, and it is easy to lose sight of fundamental questions such as:

- What rate of return does your business require to survive and develop?
- What changes are taking place in the business of our competitors and our markets?
- How can our business best produce and deliver the products and services which our customers want?

Influences on Business Objectives

No two firms will set the same objectives because what a business wants to achieve in a forthcoming budget period will be influenced by:
- the history and current preferences of the business;
- its skills and know-how;
- the resources it can command.

Examples of Business Objectives

1. **General**
   a) achieve growth and reduce risk;
   b) diversity into new markets and products to reduce the risk attendant on too great a reliance on a limited range of products;

c) concentrate on areas of expertise;

d) rationalise product streams and sourcing.

2. Marketing

a) achieve a defined percentage growth in sales;

b) improve market share from the present position;

c) widen the product range;

d) move into new markets and locations.

3. Financial

a) increase operating profits to a defined percentage;

b) increase return on investment by a defined rate;

c) maximise use of existing assets;

d) reduce debt equity ratio to a predefined level.

4. Organisational

a) decentralise/centralise;

b) review managerial responsibilities and accountability;

c) review personnel performance assessment and reward policies;

d) introduce more democratic management style.

> **WORD TO THE WISE**
> The necessary review of the current state of your business should be carried out in an atmosphere of honesty and realism and the process of review must include all parts of the business which affect its capacity to deliver what your customer requires.

When selecting your objectives, remember to:

- set objectives for what matters most;

- set objectives with which you and your business can cope;

- set broad team or departmental objectives and allow scope for individual contributions;

> • set your objectives in measurable terms so that you can make the assessment of your progress part of the budgeting process.

Ways of Expressing Objectives

The objectives must be expressed in terms that make sense for each one. For example, they can be stated in the following ways.

- In absolute terms, such as sales to reach £2 million.
- In relative terms, such as sales to increase 10 per cent on the current year.
- As a range, such as percentage of stock to sales to be between 10 per cent and 15 per cent.
- As a ratio, such as return on total assets to be 16 per cent.
- As a maximum, such as debt equity ratio not to exceed 50 per cent.
- As a minimum, such as dividend cover of at least twice.

The Key Role of Financial Objectives in Budgeting

Other objectives may be just as important to business success but clear financial objectives are key indicators of business achievement and are essential to effective budget planning. Financial objectives must be:

(a) set in the guidelines issued at the start of the budgeting process;

(b) incorporated in the summary or master budget where the profit and loss accounts and balance sheets show the financial objectives to be achieved in the budget period;

(c) worked through systematically into the budgets for income, expenses, liabilities and asset deployment which are prepared in detail during the budgeting process;

(d) monitored throughout the budget period, in detail, at all budget levels, so that management can show how the financial objectives are in fact being achieved.

Financial Budgeting Objectives

The budget objectives should be the financial criteria used to judge the performance of the company. These can normally be calculated from the profit and loss accounts and balance sheet information. Some examples are given below.

1. Profitability

a) *earnings per share*: the company will earn 25p per share in the upcoming budget period, compared to 20p per share in the current year;

b) *return on total assets*: the company will earn 15 per cent on total assets employed, compared to 14 per cent in the current year;

c) *before and after tax earnings*: earnings before tax will be £10,000 and the expected average tax rate is 30 per cent, giving after tax profits of £7,000;

d) *fixed costs*: fixed costs will be contained at £12,000, down from £14,000 in the current year;

e) *sales, variable costs and margin on sales*: sales will rise to £100,000 in the budget year compared to £85,000 in the current year. Variable costs will remain at 78 per cent, i.e. £78,000 in the budget year and margins at 22 per cent, giving a budgeted gross margin of £22,000.

2. Liquidity

a) *payment and collection periods*: payment will average 36.5 days, and collections 45.5 days,

b) *stock ratio*: stocks will average 36.5 days;

c) *debt/equity ratios*: the company will maintain debt of at least 30 per cent of equity but not more than 50 per cent. On an equity of £200,000 this means borrowings will be at least £60,000 and not more than £100,000.

3. Activity

a) *asset turnover rate*: the rate will not fall below the current rate of 0.3 times per year;

b) *sales per day*: sales will rise from £130,000 per day to £174,000 per day.

The Financial Budgets

The financial budgets normally comprise of:
- a profit and loss account;
- the cash flow statement;
- the balance sheet.

Contents of Financial Budgets

The budgeted profit and loss account, balance sheet and cash flow forecasts must contain all the significant elements of income, expenses, operating expenditure, liabilities and assets which determine whether the financial objectives will be achieved.

For instance, if the key financial objective is to achieve earnings of 100p per share, then the earnings figure will come from the profit and loss account and the number of shares during the budget period from the balance sheet. To establish responsibilities for income and expenses, the budgeted profit and loss account must show the various main sources of revenue, less the

> **WORD TO THE WISE**
>
> Setting objectives for your business allows you to define your aspirations in ways that you can use to measure against the business. You will achieve much more by remembering to balance what is achievable with what is aspirational in the objectives you set for yourself and all of the business.

matching expenses charged against them. The balance sheet will disclose the shareholders' equity, assets employed and liabilities and again it must be clear where the responsibility for these items lies.

STEP 4: DECIDE ON THE BUDGET APPROACH

It is necessary to consider what type of budgeting approach you are now going to use to convert your objectives into the formal financial budget.

Zero-base Budgeting

Zero-base budgeting starts from the assumption that levels of expenditure in a previous period do not justify continuation of that spending in future periods. All spending must be justified from scratch each year. Zero-base budgeting is most useful in control of indirect, overhead activities.

The advantages claimed for zero-base budgeting are that it:

- forces examination of all current service and support activities in the light of business objectives and strategies, not just new proposals;

- looks for alternative ways of performing activities and eliminates activities which are no longer necessary;

- identifies the resources required to perform activities at various levels of priority;

- is effective in ranking all activities in terms of importance and securing optimum allocation of scarce resources.

With zero-base budgeting, the whole of the existing business base is examined. This means that every item in the budget has to be justified as though the particular activity or programme were starting anew. Priorities and preferences might then be re-established in terms of the business and financial objectives. Obsolete and underperforming pro-grammes could be isolated so that resources could be deployed elsewhere.

As a concept zero-base budgeting has therefore much to commend it, but against this must be weighted its practical limitations. To examine thoroughly every item in the budget and every underlying activity or programme would probably be impossible.

Nevertheless, in spite of the practical limitations of zero-base budgeting and in spite of it imposing a highly rational approach to budgeting on organisations that are essentially complex, interest in zero-base budgeting still remains. When faced with continuous limitations and reductions in their level of spending, organisations might be expected to look for more efficient ways of spreading the impact of those reductions than simply requiring every service to take the same across-the-board cut.

To overcome the administrative burden of a pure zero-base budgeting system, you may consider using it on selected products, projects, departments or activities in your business, so that, over a 3 or 5 year period, all the critical areas have been the subject of this useful approach.

Incremental Budgeting

Many people and organisations work on the assumption that budgets will grow each year. The rationalisations for this may be to allow for inflation or to provide for 'natural growth'. Incremental budgeting is the general approach in governmental budgeting but is also found in private industry, especially in indirect functions, such as planning

and research. The approach is criticised from the
scientific management and the systems point of
view because it does not relate spending to the work
to be accomplished. It may also avoid scrutiny of all
activities to see whether they are required or not.

Which to Choose?

If you have carried out a good review of your business and have set your objectives, will you will be
able to take elements of these two approaches and
give a realistic basis on which to build your budget.
In other words, you need to consider:

* that nothing you do in your existing business
  practice is justified "just because you've always
  done it";
* that you can use your existing practices, which
  you have reviewed and assessed as being appropriate to your business objectives, as a sound
  and reasonable basis for setting future targets.

REMEMBER

DO:

- Use the knowledge and expertise existing in your workforce in your business review and planning.

- Check the expectations of your customers against your own business expectations. If yours do not relate to your customers you need to redefine your objectives and targets. Set your objectives for what matters most – your customers.

- Give sufficient time to the planning stage of the budget process. You will not succeed in budgeting without clear objectives.

DO NOT:

- Restrict your objectives to just finance. There are significant other objectives which must be set in order to develop your business and make a sound basis for the future.

- Be afraid to recognise what you and your business can cope with. By looking at your current limits you can come up with ideas on how to overcome them and expand your capabilities for the future.

Chapter 3

Budget Preparation

This chapter will help you to:

- know how to do all the important work of quantifying in detail your budget plan in terms of money and other targets;

- gather vital information and co-ordinate your budget guidelines and assumptions as part of a budget structure;

- understand key definitions of terms you will come across when setting your own budget.

Budget Preparation

You are now at the stage where you have set and agreed you business and financial objectives and are ready to physically prepare the budgets. With the understanding you have gained, particularly from the review process, you can move on to prepare a forecast, whether for sales, production, capital expenditure for your own particular department.

The all-important preparatory work consists of three main stages.

1. Gathering information.

2. Co-ordinating the key assumptions.

3. Creating the budget forms.

Each stage is of equal significance and should be given the same amount of attention.

GATHERING INFORMATION

The background information that you need to accumulate and how and where you obtain it will vary according to your individual requirements and circumstances. Nevertheless, there are some common areas which are applicable to most situations.

- The limiting factor.
- External influences.
- Internal influences.
- Sources of advice.

WORD TO THE WISE

The quality of the effort you put in to the all-important preparation work will be a critical factor in how successful your budget setting will be.

The Limiting Factor

Although it sounds rather theoretical, the idea of a 'limiting factor' is a very real and practical one. The phrase simply refers to a key, overriding influence which has a significant, constraining effect upon your business. There may be only one, or there may be a number of limiting factors affecting your business. You need to identify for yourself what the limiting factors are in your business.

The following are examples of typical limiting factors. Consider which one, if any, are applicable to you.

- A lack of funds available for expanding sales and/or production levels, purchasing new capital items and so on.

- A shortage of labour or up to date equipment and machinery will affect production and subsequent sales budgets.

- A small and stagnant marketplace will act as a limit on potential sales

- In a service company a skills shortage – the maximum number of skilled hours you can sell is determined by the number of labour hours available to you.

- A scarcity or irregular supply of raw materials may be a limiting factor on production levels – and therefore upon sales, volume and ultimately, profit.

- The sales volume potential of a hotel or restaurant is limited by its bed or table capacity (in the absence of capacity expansion). The opportunity to increase volume lies only in improving the occupancy rate or table turnover.

- An absence of planning permission to physically expand and therefore to diversify.

- A monopolistic marketplace, dominated by one or two powerful competitors.
- Competition laws.
- The objectives of the organisation as set out in the memorandum and articles of association.
- Quotas operating on import or export of raw materials or finished goods.
- Existing patents.

As you think about the limiting factors that are most applicable to you, it will become evident that you do need to have a broad knowledge and understanding of what is going on around you in your business now and during the forthcoming period. Only then can you hope to produce a relatively accurate budget forecast that takes account of all the key circumstances. Accordingly, you will have to draw regularly on the numerous sources of information available to you.

External Influences

Conscious of the overall constraint upon your sales, production, capital expenditure, departmental budget or whatever, you should contemplate and list for future reference all of the possible external influences which may have some effect on your particular budget and its revenues and expenditure.

Again, these will depend on your given situation but might include: rivals' products, activities and strategies and economic factors, such as inflation or interest rates.

The following are some of the numerous external factors that may be relevant to your circumstances.

- Inflation.
- Interest rates.

- Government monetary policy.
- Tax legislation.
- Economy cycle.
- Suppliers' terms and conditions.
- Suppliers' location.
- Competitors' strategies.
- Labour wage demands.
- Labour training supply.
- Population growth trends.
- Exchange regulations.
- Environmental issues.

There are many sources of information available to you to help you to consider the external factors relevant to you, largely because of the great range and diversity of influences that exist. Talk to customers and suppliers, obtain competitors' literature, perhaps by subscribing to their mailing lists, approach trade bodies, reading their newsletters and attending their conferences, seminars and exhibitions

Read widely – general and business newspapers and magazines, specific documents, such as government and EU publications. Use consultants, job centres, employment agencies and local authorities as sources of information. Know enough to make educated guesses and, most importantly, where to go for a second opinion.

Internal Influences

You should be aware of all the internal influences that exist within your business or department, those which may have a beneficial or adverse effect upon your upcoming budget.

Items, such as stock level requirements, employees' wage demands and, other departmental budgets would have a significant influence on your budget setting.

The following are some of the internal influences that may be of relevance to your business.

- Existing contracts to supply.
- Employee demands.
- Marketing strategy.
- Cash resources.
- Channels of distribution.
- Pricing policies.
- Agreed terms and conditions.
- Physical assets condition.
- Capital replacement requirements.
- Key management changes.
- Personnel policies.

Sources of Advice

You must inform yourself about what the important internal factors are in your business.

The following are some of the sources of advice that may be available to your business.

- Attending meetings.
- Asking questions.
- Talking to directors, shareholders, colleagues and employees.
- Reading memoranda, reports and other documents rather than skimming them or putting them to one side.

You have to keep your eyes and ears open permanently, soaking up what is occurring now and all the ifs, buts and maybes of what could take place in the future. If you are using the team approach to gather the information you have far more opportunity to ensure that the budget process will consider all the relevant internal factors.

For an existing business the most important internal information is considered to be the current and historic income, expenditure, profitability and net asset status. This makes the current year's trading statements plus a forecast to complete the accounting period a critical piece of management information. It is vital, however, to remember the outcomes of your business review and the objectives you have set – do not limit your horizons by considering only the current picture.

CO-ORDINATE THE ASSUMPTIONS

Having built up extensive preparatory notes, you should now be in a position to press ahead and actually compile the budget for your department or business. To do this, you need to concentrate on creating the form for it, accumulating the contents and producing the final version – only then can you expect to prepare a budget which incorporates all the elements necessary.

Budget guidelines should start with a statement of the main factors expected to effect the business in the coming period.

These factors include:
• pricing strategy;
• rate of inflation expected to apply;
• labour cost fluctuations and timing;
• interest rates;
• timing issues on income volumes;

- anticipated payment timings for customers and suppliers;
- employee numbers.

The guidelines should state the performance required from each department.

For example:
- key financial ratios;
- the required net earnings;
- for each department or profit centre, the required return on assets employed.

The guidelines should clearly set out the standard definitions to be used in the budgets.

Standard definitions of income, expense, asset and liabilities must be established from the start. These definitions will be applied throughout the budgeting process, from the outline budget statement produced to the draft budgets, the final budgets set and finally to the actual results monitored against budget.

If definitions change the players will complain that the goal posts are being moved. Having said that, it is a fact that few organisations get all their definitions settled at the first try. What happens is that a working definition is first established and this is refined as problems are encountered. In this case, it is important that everyone understands the changes made.

BELOW IS A LIST OF SOME DEFINITIONS
Sales Volumes
- Sales volumes will be expressed in a common unit as far as possible. For example, a consultancy will define volumes in terms of chargeable hours, while a steel manufacturer will express volumes in terms of tons.

- Volumes should be net of returns.
- The product range will be grouped by agreed categories so that summaries are on a consistent basis over time.
- Not all sections of the business will use the same unit, for example, a hotel will express volume in terms of bed occupancy, restaurant orders and bar takings.

Sales Revenues

Sales revenues can be defined as the amounts receivable for goods and services supplied, but this definition needs to be clarified to show which items are or are not a part of the sales revenues.

Items which should be accounted for separately are:
- duties, such as VAT, customs and excise duties;
- sales within the group;
- technical service fees and royalties receivable;
- cash discounts
- sales of by-products and scrap;
- recharging of costs between departments.

Items which are likely to be excluded are:
- sales of fixed assets;
- investment income;
- interest receivable.

Variable Costs

The variable costs should be defined as those costs which vary directly with output and/or turnover. These are also known as 'direct costs' or *'direct expenditure'*. For most companies this includes:

- raw materials;
- bought-in components;

- an element of distribution costs;
- direct labour may be treated as a variable cost. Remember it may be variable with sales or production volumes in volume stages rather than absolute numbers;
- Some elements of sales and marketing costs.

Fixed Costs

The fixed costs should be defined as those, which are not directly related to production/sales or activity levels. Also known as '*indirect expenditure*' or '*overheads*'. These costs cover areas such as:
- rents and rates;
- financing costs;
- general site services.

Capital Expenditure

Expenditure on non-consumable items of long-term use to the business. Some businesses would set a minimum value on what expenditure is to be regarded as capital, e.g £1,000.

Profits

The various definitions of profit or margin should relate to the appropriate stages at which each appears in the budget statement, for example:

- Revenues less selling costs = sales margin.
- Sales margin less variable costs = gross margin.
- Gross margin less manufacturing fixed cost = margin on manufacturing.
- Gross margin less overheads = net profit on operations (non-manufacturing business).
- Net profit on operations less interest = net profit.
- Net profit less tax = net earnings to shareholders.

CREATING THE BUDGET FORMS

The budget form is the actual layout you will use to set out the necessary financial and non-financial information making up your budget. Some organisations provide standardised budget forecast forms to be completed, most notably for sales, production and capital expenditure. Others allow their departmental managers, or whoever is responsible for filling them in, to create their own documents, which may be more appropriate, as circumstances can vary considerably from one department to another.

Whatever your situation, it is sensible to be aware of the main do's and don'ts of composing or perhaps amending (sometimes quite substantially) a budget forecast form.

Ideally, your form should be:
- basic and clear;
- attractive;
- compatible.

Basic and Clear

Keep the form as simple and as straightforward as you can, so that you are able to complete it comfortably and colleagues can understand it easily. Put in only those major revenue and/or expenditure headings which need to be included, such as 'direct expenditure' and 'indirect expenditure' in a departmental forecast. Place them in a logical and progressive order.

You should consider excluding individual subheadings, such as 'rent', 'rates', 'water' and 'heat, light and power', as these may not have to be filled in every time and could, therefore, either clutter the form unnecessarily and/or be confusing. Leave sufficient room for relevant sub-headings to be added by the person completing the form, where appropriate.

Attractive

You must ensure that your budget forecast form is not only basic but attractive too, so that it helps to present the right image – of a well-thought out and carefully prepared, professional proposal.

Make certain it is spacious, so that figures can be set apart and will therefore be distinguishable and easy to read. Avoid the use of colour, different or unusual typefaces, highlighted or shaded areas, as these tend to distract or even muddle the reader.

Try not to add more than brief explanatory notes, perhaps about how to complete the form (if a colleague is to do it for you) and any key assumptions, such as the anticipated rates of interest and inflation that have been (or should be) taken into account. Remember though, a lot of notes can be off-putting.

Compatible

Choose a standardised layout, typeface and comparable headings and categories, for comparison purposes. You must ensure that the headings for income, expenditure, assets and liabilities used are compatible with your existing management and financial reporting. This includes ensuring compatibility with the cost centres and account headings in the general ledger that create your financial accounts.

In an organisation where your budget is one of a number of different departmental budgets, compatibility is very important. Make sure that your budget form is similar to those drawn up for other departments, as this will stand it in good stead during budget discussions and enable information to be taken from it easily for master budget calculations.

It is also important to use compatible terminology with common practice in your business – you will confuse and frustrate if you budget refers to 'inventory' or 'receivables' when your business has always referred to 'stock' and 'debtors'.

Your business size and complexity will determine what budget forms you will decide to use. It is important to remember that the forms could, and should, be adapted for changing circumstances and needs. You must see the form as an aid to your budgeting not a constraint.

PREPARING A DRAFT BUDGET

It is useful to consider again the stages of budget preparation which you have now covered.

The preparation of budgets goes through a number of stages at which drafts are prepared and then amended in the light of discussions between managers, subordinates, departments and functions. The following sequence is typical.

1. Timetable

Prepare and circulate a timetable to involved persons.

2. Key factors

Identify the key commercial factors which will affect the business in the budget period. This involves analysing the potential markets for products, activities and competitors, and planned new product introductions. The whole strategic position of the company should be considered.

3. Guidelines

Prepare, a set of guidelines stating the key budget factors and conditions which will apply in the budget period. A tentative statement of financial

performance must be included. The key financial ratios should reflect the commercial factors
impacting the business. Some, such as trading
profit to turnover are in general use, others will
be specific, such as contribution per square foot
in retailing or gross margin for process industries.

4. Prepare draft budgets

This will involve expressing the overall guidelines
into the factors affecting particular departments,
such as trends in quantity, discounts, debtor
days outstanding, shipment delays and so on.

Where at all possible, the drafts will be prepared to conform to the overall guidelines, but
where, after discussions and analysis, the drafts
do not conform to guidelines, explanations
should be prepared, along with statements showing the effects that conformity to guidelines
would have on commercial performance, costs,
revenues and assets employed.

It will be useful to combine the review of current budgets against actual performance with
the preparation of new budgets.

Those setting the budget should anticipate any
problems likely to affect profits and some
allowances may have to be made for contingencies
such as a downturn in sales after devaluation in a
Third World country or a strike over a pay award.

5. Draft budget review

The draft should be checked to ensure conformity with long-term plans, all business and financial objectives and the budget guidelines. The
review checks that:
- expenditure is within cash flow limits;
- individual department budgets are co-ordinated
  to the centre.

6. Prepare master budget

It is most likely that a business manager or finance person will prepare the consolidated draft master budget with accompanying financial statements including the calculation of financial performance and other ratios.

WHAT IS A MASTER BUDGET

A master budget summarises the objectives of all sub-units of an organisation – sales, production, distribution and finance. It quantifies the expectations regarding future income, cash flows, financial status and supporting plans. The master budget is the financial model that describes the organisation, its objectives, its inputs and its outputs.

FIGURE 3.1 PROFIT + LOSS ACCOUNT BUDGET

Budget Form A
Basic Example

Budget Period: _____

PROFIT BUDGET	JAN	FEB	MAR	APR	MAY	JUN	JUL	AUG	SEP	OCT	NOV	DEC	TOTAL
Sales (A)													
Less: Direct Costs													
Cost of Materials													
Wages – Direct													
Gross Profit (B)													
Gross Profit Margin (A − B x 100%)													
Overheads													
Salaries													
Rent, Rates, Water													
Insurance													
Repairs, Renewals													
Heat, Light, Power													
Postage													
Printing, Stationary													
Transport													
Telephone													
Professional Fees													
Interest Charges													
Other													
Total Overheads (C)													
Trading Profit (B − C)													
Less Depreciation													
Net Profit Before Tax													

Date Prepared: _____

Draft No: _____

REMEMBER

DO;

- Use a range of information, both internal and external, to set your guidelines and objectives.

- Create the budget forms to suit your business definitions and needs.

- Review the individual budgets as you go along. Check that they conform to the guidelines and objectives.

DO NOT:

- Neglect any of the stages of budget preparation – information gathering, setting guidelines, assumption and creating the budget form – all are equally important and your budget will be flawed if you do.

Chapter 4

Preparing Income And Expenditure Budgets

This chapter will help you to:

- produce a sales/income and a cost budget for your business;

- relate the income and expenditure structure of the business to your strategic plan;

- produce the necessary budgets you will use in managing your business;

- decide what type of income and expenditure you should focus on and include in your formal budget.

Preparing Income and Expenditure Budgets

PART 1: PREPARING INCOME BUDGETS

For a commercial organisation, the sales or income budget is usually the first to be drafted, evaluated and agreed upon in the course of budget preparation. The reason is that sales achievement determines the practicability of all other budgets. If you can't sell, you are not in business.

Basis of the Income Budget

The analysis required to substantiate income budgets can be summarised as follows:

- define the markets for the company's product(s);
- analyse the demand characteristics of the market(s) for the product(s);
- analyse the supply characteristics of the product(s) market(s);
- determine the market shares which the company can reasonably expect to obtain for each product or product group;
- prepare the income or sales budget from volumes and prices predicted on the basis of the foregoing analyses.

Relate the Income Budget to your Strategic Plan

The starting point for the short-term budget may be the estimates of markets, market shares and income produced as part of the company's strategic planning process, but the plan for the coming

WORD TO THE WISE
Ensure that the budget set is both challenging and realistic.

budget period will require far more detailed analysis
as the strategy figures are updated in the light of new
information becoming available.

In some product areas, the short-term budget
may plan for higher targets than were envisaged in
the strategic plan. In others, progress may be slow-
er. Some product markets may be affected by new
factors, such as innovations in technology which
require re-tooling or new product developments.

The Sales Plan

The sales or income budgets are normally based on a
sales plan. The plans are divided into three sections.
1. The plan to achieve overall business and marketing objectives.
2. The trade plan.
3. The organisational plan.

The plan to achieve overall business and marketing objectives

This plan makes clear how the sales plan will meet
the business and marketing objectives of your
organisation and will form the basis of a clear marketing strategy.

The trade plan

This plan identifies the key tasks and plans for han-
dling all customers and competitors. Specific attention is given to:
• key account plans;
• prices, margins and discounting plans;
• trade promotional objectives;
• quality control and servicing objectives;
• relationships with retail outlets;
• plans for meeting competition.

The organisational plan

This section deals with any planned internal organisational changes and developments necessary to

achieve the sales plan of the business. It will incorporate the costs of benefits of training plans and the implementation of operational standards for the sales force.

SALES VOLUME

The estimates of sales volumes must be made according to the sectors in which various products are competing. The starting point will be existing markets, which may increase or fall. Then the company share of the market will be estimated. Market share may also rise or fall, although not as a simple reflection of the total market. For example, a falling market may be expected to eliminate competitors and lead to a rising market share. Within these overall targets, individual products may give increasing or decreasing sales volumes according to the competition and the stage in the product life cycle.

The current market for Product X and its competitors is 50,000 units and Product X sells 20 per cent of the market, i.e. 10,000 units. The market is expected to fall by 20 per cent in the budget year, to 40,000 units, but Product X will increase its market share to 30 per cent, that is 12,000 units.

Pricing and Sales Volumes

Sales volumes and prices go together and should be estimated together. The volume of sales will depend on the following.

- The competitive situation.
- Spending on the promotion of the products or services.
- The stage in the life cycle of all products.
- The type of sale expected.
- Cannibalisation.

The Product Life Cycle

The market potential and profitability of products change over time. The product life cycle identifies four stages.

Competitive Stages

The three competitive stages in the development of a market for your product or service market or service can be identified.

1. The product pioneer is the sole supplier with 100 per cent of the or service and production capacity.
2. Competitors penetrate the market and leader's share of market and production capacity fall, but sales volumes may still be rising as the market grows.

   Competitors may set lower prices which customers may perceive as reflecting risks of uncertain quality.

   The leader loses perceived quality premium and with it any price premium.

   Capacity becomes too large for the market and margins decline, thus keeping out new entrants and leading to Stage 3.
3. Market shares, prices and production capacity stabilise. Some competitors may withdraw and the market leader may drive for a higher market share. Rates of profitability fall to an average rate.

STAGES OF A PRODUCT LIFE CYCLE

Introduction. At the introductory stage, sales are slow and markets and profits limited because of high investment and promotion costs.

Market growth. At this stage, sales grow, markets are widened and profits improve.

Maturity. At this stage, sales grow little, if at all. Profits stabilise or begin to decline and may be defended by heavy marketing expenditures or the products may be regarded as 'cash cows' to be milked whilst resources are concentrated on 'new stars'

Decline. At this stage, the product begins to lose its appeal in the face of new entrants to the market or competing new products, changing public taste and fashion. Sales decline, the market contracts or is divided into a growing number of companies and profits fall.

While it is sometimes difficult to establish exactly where you are in the different stages of the cycle, nevertheless the idea of the life cycle does highlight the need to continuously review:
• sales performance of all products;
• profit performance of all products;
• marketing, production and purchasing policies.

Price and Promotion Spending

The price the customer is asked to pay is related to the amount the company is prepared to pay on promotion of the product. Four strategies are possible.

1. **High price/high promotion spending**
   This strategy uses high promotional spending to:
   • give rapid market penetration;
   • build up brand preference before the entry of competitors;
   • achieve early profit and cash breakeven.

2. **High price/low promotion spending**
   This strategy:
   • gives high profit combined with low promotion costs;

- suits a small, price insensitive market, insulated from competition;
- does not suit promotion of a new product or concept in a widely based consumer market.

3. Low price/high promotion spending
This strategy is advisable when:
- the market is large;
- large-scale production with falling marginal unit costs are obtainable;
- the market is new but buyers are expected to be price sensitive;
- early copying or imitation will lead to rapid entry of competitors.

4. Low price/low promotion spending
This strategy works best when:
- there is a large, price sensitive market;
- the market is not very sensitive to promotion;
- in a well-established market.

Type of Sale
Volume and prices may also depend on the type of sale. Sales may fall into any of the following categories.

1. First-time sales
In this case, sales volumes depend on the size of the total market and the share of market achieved in each time period.

2. Replacement sales
These will depend on the life of the first product sold, whether it gives satisfaction, the availability of substitutes from competitors, market and fashion trends, selling effort and so on. Some businesses ignore replacement sales until the product is well established and some clear idea of the market emerges. The profitability of replacement sales can be better than first-time sales where promo-

tional spend has been high. The quality of your service or product will re-sell for you.

3. **Repeat sales**
   Some products, such as food and drink, are purchased repeatedly. Since the unit price is usually low, the rate of repeat purchase is an important determinant of sales volume.

4. **Spares**
   For some products, such as aircraft, the market for spares may be captured with the initial sale and may actually be equivalent to a further two or three aircraft sales over a future time period. In the case of most cars, however, the spares market is not usually captured entirely by the initial sale.

Cannibalisation

It is essential to judge the effect of marketing new products on the existing product line. New products may have some attributes in common with existing lines.

1. **All aspects of new products should be challenged individually and in total.** For instance, where there are already two products and a third is introduced, the total contribution of all three should normally exceed that of the two unless there are strategic reasons for the third product to be introduced as a 'loss leader'.

2. **Your marketing department should be asked to produce arguments for and against a new product.**

3. **A new product may be tested for 'product steal'** (i.e. the extent to which is will replace sales of other products) before launch as part of the market research at the test market stage.

4. **The impact analysis should quantify the financial implication of the new product introduction.**

This detailed type of anaysis may seem excessive where you feel you have been adequately setting your budgets each year based on 'last year's figure plus a percentage'. The value of the work cannot be underestimated. The questions, awareness and focus that it will generate for you will definately lead to both a better budget and a plan of action for the future.

PART 2: PREPARING EXPENDITURE BUDGETS

It is wise to consider your expenditure under three headings.

1. Types.
2. Amounts.
3. Timings.

TYPES

Whether you are composing a production, capital expenditure or departmental budget forecast for finance, administration, etc., there are various types of expenditure that may apply to your circumstances.

If accurate planning, monitoring and controlling are to be carried out, it is advisable to divide expenditure into at least four types – 'start-up', 'direct', 'indirect' and 'capital'.

Start-up Expenditure

Start-up expenditure encompasses those costs that are incurred purely as a consequence of doing, producing or selling something for the first time. Introducing a new product is an obvious example of this. So, too, would be moving into another market sector to trade. Thus, these expenses might include producing drawings and specifications for that new item, establishing a production line, rewriting and reprinting sales brochures, catalogues and so on.

In effect, any 'one-off' costs could fit under this broad heading.

Direct Expenditure

Direct expenditure is that which varies directly with production and/or sales levels and incorporates costs for items such as raw materials, component parts, goods for resale, labour and distribution costs. Basically, if production and/or sales levels rise, then so do direct costs as more of these items are used up too – and vice versa when production and/or sales levels fall. Direct costs are also often known as '*variable costs*'.

Indirect Expenditure

Indirect expenditure covers all of those costs which are incurred by a business on a regular basis, but are not linked directly to production and/or sales and do not vary in the short-term with volume. Thus, these will include expenditure on rent, communication, etc. However many products are being manufactured and services provided, these costs will still have to be paid. Sometimes, indirect costs are referred to as '*fixed costs*' or '*overheads*'.

Capital Expenditure

Capital expenditure – somewhat obviously – is expenditure on non-consumable items of long-term, permanent use to a business. Buildings, plant, equipment, machinery and vehicles can be classified in this way. Most businesses will set a threshold figure of perhaps £1,000, above which items will be classified as capital expenditure, and below which they will be categorised under another heading, such as overheads. Not surprisingly, capital items will depreciate in value with time and usage and any good budgeting structure will incorporate a plan for their replacement over time.

HOW TO DECIDE WHAT TYPE OF EXPENDITURE TO INCLUDE

As with the different types of revenue, you need to decide for yourself how you are going to subdivide these four categories – obviously, it will depend mainly on your own circumstances and the costs that are most likely to be incurred in your budget. It is also essential that the headings and sub-headings used are the same throughout the organisation in order to avoid confusion, especially when the master budget is consequently pulled together. The following checklist of these headings and numerous sub-headings, may assist you.

Start-up Expenditure	Indirect Expenditure
Drawings	Rent
Specifications	Heat, light, power
Production line	Insurance
Rewriting literature	Maintenance
Reprinting literature	Indirect staff costs
Promotional costs	Advertising
	Telephones
	Professional fees
	Finance charges
Direct Expenditure	**Capital Expenditure**
Raw materials	Buildings
Component parts	Plant
Goods for resale	Equipment
Labour wages	Machinery
After-sales service	Vehicles
Distribution costs	Patents

AMOUNTS

You need to contemplate expenditure both in terms of quantities and prices paid.

Start-up Costs

Start-up costs associated with a new project are often the hardest to calculate, but you must rely on the quality of your business review and information gathering process.

Direct Costs

Direct costs tend to be easier to estimate than start-up expenditure because they are related so closely to the sales levels that have been established for your income budget.

Thus, to calculate the quantities of raw materials, component parts and so forth that are likely to be needed for the period, you should refer to the relevant budgets in order to note down these figures. From there, it should be a relatively straightforward task to look at production and labour records to date to evaluate the quantities of direct materials, labour and equipment used at these levels of production. Think about external and internal factors as well – maybe stock level requirements need to be higher or lower at the end of the period.

Similarly, it is possible to anticipate the prices to be paid for certain quantities of direct materials, labour, etc., based again on your budget guidelines. Obviously, you have to take account of the varying prices at different levels of sales and output, allowing for bulk buy discounts, overtime rates and so forth. Budget for external and internal influences as usual: for example, seasonal shortages of raw materials and upcoming strikes by overseas dockworkers when you are awaiting supplies of imported component parts will be detrimental.

Indirect Expenditure

You should be able to estimate most indirect expenditure with more ease. You should be especially conscious here of external and internal factors, which can have a noticeable impact – such as the introduction of more stringent health and safety guidelines for your industry, which may necessitate additional repairs to, and maintenance of, your premises.

The actual sums handed over for indirect expenditure should be readily identifiable well in advance too – some such as rent will be fixed, whilst others, such as electricity and gas for heat, light and power can be calculated by looking at the respective unit costs for the preceding period, allowing for any expected increases due and then working out the overall costs in relation to the units used. Again, be aware of external and internal influences – the opportunity to obtain electricity, gas and telephone supplies from other, more competitively priced sources, for example, may arise.

Capital Expenditure

Capital expenditure on items such as equipment, machinery and vehicles will almost definitely be the easiest to estimate because these goods are bought infrequently and planned for many months or, more likely, years ahead. Chat to fellow departmental heads, study investment appraisal and depreciation figures for items purchased some time ago and see which have been scheduled for replacement in this period. Pay extra attention to those external and internal factors here – rapidly developing technology, increased sales and production demands and the introduction of new goods can all affect capital stock requirements. Also consider the physical condition of existing assets and evaluate what risk exists of items needing unplanned replacement because of failure and breakdown.

TIMING

The timing of start-up, direct, indirect and capital expenditures must be planned carefully so that they co-ordinate well with the amounts and timings of your incoming revenues.

In short, you must ensure that expenditure does not precede revenues unless absolutely necessary. If such a situation is allowed to persist, the business will encounter the considerable risk of running out of cash and perhaps even being forced to close, despite any underlying profitability. The smaller the firm and the fewer the resources, the likelier this is to happen. Consider this timing issue carefully. While you can use working capital to fund short-term cash needs, it is always wiser to try and match the timing of revenue and expenditure to limit both your finance cost and your business risk.

Start-up Expenditure

Start-up expenditure will inevitably be incurred before any revenues can be recouped from the new product, diversification, etc.

Direct Expenditure

The timing of direct expenditure on raw materials, component parts, labour or whatever tends to be more predictable as you will know what you require and when, by looking at your sales and production figures and working backwards from them. Referring to those documents which detail suppliers' payment terms and conditions, your usual payment times, employees' pay days and so on, you should be able to assess payment dates with some degree of accuracy. Keep your eyes open for opportunities and risks. Early purchase at lower prices may be benefical but stockholding risks may be excessive.

Indirect Expenditure

Indirect expenditure on rent, rates, water and similar costs should be easy to schedule, with rent due perhaps quarterly, rates and water rates payable over monthly instalments and so forth. Be conscious of any appropriate influences – a revised incentive scheme may bring forward some payments to your workforce but could have a positive influence in retaining skills required for project completion.

Capital Expenditure

Not surprisingly, capital expenditure will often be the simplest to timetable into the budget forecast, because it will have been planned so far in advance in many instances. You need to speak to other departmental heads and check documents, such as investment appraisal forms to establish probable purchasing dates. External and internal factors may be most influential here though – for example, imminent technological developments may make it wise to delay a purchase.

REMEMBER

DO:

- Prepare a sales plan on which you can base your income budget.

- Consider where your products or services are currently placed in the product life cycle.

- Have a method of co-ordinating the assumption – both your income and expenditure budgets.

DO NOT:

- Be tempted to use someone else's budget model. Set the headings yourself based on your own assessment of your needs.

- Ignore the timing factor in co-ordinating your revenues and expenditure budgets. These can be critical and can have significant impact on your all-important cashflow.

Chapter 5

How To Stay In Budget

This chapter will help you to:

- understand how to use your budget to control your business;

- set up a budget control system that will actually work for your business;

- understand in practical terms how to correct variances that occur and internally improve business performance and profitability.

How to Stay In Budget

BUDGETING AS A CONTROL TOOL

The aims of a budgetary control system are to develop and implement plans, co-ordinate sections and departments and monitor performance in the light of plans. The system will only work if it is *used* by managers and supervisors and if it leads to corrective actions.

The prime objective of budgetary control is to delegate responsibility for cost control to the persons who actually commit resources and incur expenditure.

It has to be said that the word 'control' does not sit easily in a business world dominated by the currently fashionable theories of federalism, decentralisation empowerment and teamwork.

But even the most star-studded football team has to have rules to co-ordinate the efforts of the team to best effect to ensure its members play together. Teamwork does not do away with the need for discipline and control, rather it increases it, but discipline and controls have to be imposed in an entirely different way. An effective manager has to understand this principle in order to operate in this environment successfully.

The task is not an easy one because while the rules have to be accepted they cannot be rigidly enforced – staff have to buy in to them. But it's not just a question of disciplines and rules. There are also strategic pressures and the control function has somehow to balance all of these influences.

In this environment of change the classic methodology of operating appropriate control by the use of budgeting is a well-used and trusted technique.

Budgets

The budget remains the centrepiece of control, linking long and short-term planning, inputting into cash and capital expenditure planning and plotting progress against plans usually monthly, in what is often called the management accounting 'package'.

However, while the methodologies are unchanged, they are being used in an entirely different way today by leading-edge companies.

MANAGEMENT CONTROL SYSTEM

Budgetary control, including capital expenditure and cash budgeting, is at the heart of good business management systems.

A properly managed budget system answers three questions.

1. Do I have the correct plans in place: **direction checking**.

2. How is each part of the business contributing to the performance of the whole: **score card**.

3. What has affected the results in each part of the business recently, what is likely to affect them in the near future and what will be the impact: **attention directing**.

The importance of the budget, done properly and taken seriously, is that it is a forward-looking document that can serve so many purposes.

- Variances between budget and actual are the means by which senior management can monitor the business and prioritise the areas for action.

- The use of variance analysis combined with the flexed budgets and an activity based approach can enable management to identify trends and get a fix on the year-end results. When combined with regular reappraisals and forecasts, this can go some way towards guarding against unpleasant surprises.

• Performance to budget is the standard tool whereby senior management measure both business unit performance and managerial performance.

What Variances?

Essentially efficient operating control means getting the maximum possible good outputs for a given quantity of inputs, or expressed in another way, it means utilising the minimum possible inputs for a given quantity of good outputs. The input/output distinction is helpful in retaining perspective on the analysis of variances.

The key question in deciding how variances should be collected and analysed are:

• Why do we wish to identify this particular variance?
• What will we do with it after we have measured it?

If we cannot make practical use of a variance then we should not bother to compute it.

A budget should not be a straight jacket that prevents the manager looking at the overall company objectives.

Elaborate budgeting and fancy reports of variance analysis will be of little benefit if the managers responsible do not use the reports as clues for investigation of off-standard performance. The real benefits become evident when managers seize the system and the reports as the starting point for improving operations.

The variances on which you need to concentrate should be selected to discover better ways of adhering to budgets, altering budgets or of accomplishing objectives.

Having had your sales, production, capital expenditure or departmental budget approved, you should now be in a position to move on and actually monitor it on a weekly, monthly or quarterly basis, as appropriate. To do this effectively, you need to establish suitable

WORD TO THE WISE
The selection of the variances you wish to measure as part of your budgetary control should be based on a clear assessment of what the critical factors are that determine what will make your business achieve its goals.

monitoring procedures and ensure that you and your team know how to study revenues and check expenditure as and when necessary so that you are able to use the budget productively.

ESTABLISHING MONITORING PROCEDURES

In theory, once a budget has been finalised, its revenues must be achieved and expenditure must not be exceeded. Of course, this is not a realistic goal as internal and external circumstances can and do change and will have some impact on your budget, for better or worse. In practice, therefore, budgets are subject to constant review and may be adjusted where circumstances change to a sufficient degree. Nonetheless, this official goal is still something to be worked towards – otherwise there is little point in setting a budget in the first place.

To help adhere to the budget, or at least to highlight that it is not possible, you need to establish monitoring procedures which are:

- easy to administer;
- regular;

- completed at the lowest level;
- relevant.

Easy to Administer

It is essential that revenues, expenditure and the consequent profits and cash flow can be monitored easily and swiftly rather than being a difficult and time-consuming process. Hence, the data needed to monitor finances – taken from your financial information system – must be available under the same category and sub-category headings as those used in your budget form.

Just as important, data has to be readily accessible and available whenever it is required. In some instances, it may need to be taken at source, direct from sales invoices, receipts, etc. – perhaps when cash flow is poor and is being matched closely each week, or even each day; on other occasions, it will be noted from company records, books, ledgers and so on. It is imperative that these records are compiled as fast, as accurately and as clearly as is necessary for budgetary purposes.

Regular

Assuming that the data concerning revenues and expenditure are available when they are wanted, the question of how often it should be checked has to be addressed – with the answer being determined by the nature of your particular business circumstances. Once a month is fairly commonplace, although you must be flexible enough to shorten or lengthen these times if your individual situation changes substantially. It would for example be a requirement of a restaurant business that variances be examined at least weekly.

Completed at the Lowest Level

The efficient monitoring of a budget usually involves control beginning at the lowest possible level of the business organisation – that is, where the revenue was received or the expenditure incurred. Each member of the team within a particular section or department must be aware of their responsibilities in this area.

Relevant

Effective monitoring tends to follow the 'management by exception' approach, whereby the budget holder has full knowledge of his or her individual budget as agreed.

In this way, your time will be kept free for you to concentrate on other, more important activities, rather than being tied up with relatively trivial matters which often do little more than confirm that the budget is progressing as anticipated. Of course, the point at which differences – or 'variances' – are considered to be 'significant' and worthy of being referred up to you will vary from one business to another. A variation of a defined percentage in amounts is often the decisive point in most firms. Clearly, everyone has to know what is termed 'significant', if this approach is to work properly.

You need to be able to identify significant variances and recognise how to deal with them so that revenues are consequently achieved and expenditure controlled in line with expectations.

Remember not to be too defensive when assessing variances. They are a fact of business life and should not be used as a stick to beat yourself or your team with. Variances tell you something useful about your business and identify not just problems but opportunities. Be positive in your approach to your variance analysis and use the information as a pointer to action.

IDENTIFYING SIGNIFICANT VARIANCES

When working within and towards a budget, it is essential to accept the fact that however careful and thorough the planning stage may have been, your budget is still based on objective assumptions. There is always an element of subjectivity involved. Similarly, internal and external circumstances do change unexpectedly and have a positive or negative impact. Thus, the budget can rarely be wholly accurate, if at all. Significant variances – generally defined as being some percentage above or below expectations – should not necessarily be seen as a failure.

To begin with, it is important that you actually spot variances, categorise them and then try to calculate their causes in your particular circumstances. Later on you can set about assessing their likely, knock-on effects on your and other budgets and how to remedy them.

Most variances can be categorised in the following ways, with the final, somewhat unusual, category requiring as must attention as the rest:

- revenue: price variance;
- revenue: volume variance;
- revenue: timing variance;
- revenue: mix variance;
- expenditure: price variance;
- expenditure: volume variance;
- expenditure: timing variance;
- no significant variances.

Revenue: Price Variance

Clearly, any noticeable variances in revenue received is of primary concern, not only to the immediate budget holder but to the entire company as most budgetary systems are revenue-initiated and driven. Sales revenues may vary due to price adjustments. Typically, prices may have had to be reduced more than expected to help a product become established in an overseas market.

Obviously, variances in selling prices of products and services for sale tend to be most significant, having both a rollover effect on the sales budget and knock-on effects on other ones. Assuming that everything else remains the same – most notably, sales volume, direct and indirect expenditure – then increased selling prices will boost gross profit, net profit and generate more cash. Evidently, the consequences will be reversed if selling prices decrease, so too will profits and immediate cash resources.

> **WORD TO THE WISE** The analysis of variances in income and expenditure against your budget will not help you achieve improvement unless the analysis is followed by action.

An increase in selling prices will generally be regarded as acceptable by most companies if (and it is sometimes as big 'if') they can be sustained and do not have an adverse effect upon sales volumes. Likewise, a drop in selling prices will be considered to be unacceptable and the remedies might include raising the prices of goods in other product groups, territories or markets in order to compensate. If this is not possible, attention may be given to nullifying the potential knock-on effects by attempting to improve sales volumes or to reduce direct and perhaps indirect expenditure so that profits and cash flow are maintained.

Revenue: Volume Variance

This is probably the most common variance of all, especially for sales revenue where the number of units sold or services provided are fewer (or occasionally more) than expected. For example, a leading customer's business may have been forced to close, with little or no warning. Alternatively, several new customers could have started trading with your firm.

Higher sales volumes will probably be viewed as a positive trend in the majority of companies, assuming that they can cope with the extra demand for goods and services. Do not forget however that you need to take action to cope with increased demand. Reduced volumes are seen as potentially fatal, especially if the downward trend continues for any length of time. Remedies might incorporate the introduction of a discount structure for bulk purchases and an advertising campaign to increase awareness of the product's strengths. If unsuccessful, thought will need to be given to reducing the impact of the variances, possibly by raising selling prices of popular lines or cutting back on expenditure, thus upholding profits and cash resources.

Revenue: Timing Variance

Often overlooked, particularly at sectional or departmental budget level where the importance of a positive cash flow is not always so apparent, is the question of the timing of the revenue obtained. In some instances, it may be received earlier – perhaps more customers than expected take advantage of a new, prompt-payment discount structure for example. On other occasions, it will be obtained later – a typical example of this is generally deteriorating economic conditions persuading customers to hold on to their money for much longer. Where a sales timing variance occurs, you may need to take corrective action to change the timing of your costs to equalise the situation.

Revenue: Mix Variance

In an environment where your pricing strategy is different for different products or product groups, this can be a vital variance to track. If you have minimum margin products within your portfolio and adverse mix variance will mean that the balance of the sales volume has shifted unfavourably to the low margin products. Significant decisions may need to be made about stopping some sales or

production. Not all sales are a good idea. It is vital
for your business that you remember this.

Solving your Negative Sales Variances

With regard to revenue price, volume and timing
variances, it is important that you always work
through the consequences in relation to your own,
individual situation. As an example, increasing the
volume of goods and services sold is normally beneficial but is not always. Perhaps the product group
that is selling more is a loss leader priced below cost
level to entice new customers to buy it. Similarly,
greater volumes may put excessive pressure on production facilities which are unable to manufacture
goods at the required rate. Also, they can pres-
surise cash resources as direct costs on raw materials and the like may have to be paid for up front.
In a service business, accepting a contract when
you do not have the resources to deliver can have a
huge impact, not just on this sale but on your rep-
utation which is so vital for future success.

Likewise, it is sensible to take account of the possible effects of any changes you might implement to
remedy those variances. For example, introducing
early settlement discounts to encourage customers
to pay more quickly may eliminate timing variances
but those taking advantage of such facilities will be
paying less, thus increasing price variances and
ultimately, reducing profit levels. Cutting credit
terms and pursuing debts can alienate and per-
suade customers to take their business elsewhere –
thus affecting price, volume and timing variances!

ACHIEVING REVENUES: AN ACTION CHECKLIST

Identifying significant revenue variances is relatively easy, as long as you adhere to your monitoring process. Resolving them and achieving revenues is harder, but referring to a checklist of points can at least help you to approach the task thoroughly and in a comprehensive manner.

	Yes	No		Yes	No
Is there a price variance?	❑	❑	Have you decided how immediate and on going to tackle it?	❑	❑
Have you considered its effects on your budget?	❑	❑	What will be the knock on effects of your response?	❑	❑
Other related budgets?	❑	❑	Do you have a problem with a timing variance?	❑	❑
Is its effect short-term?	❑	❑	Do you realise what it is doing to your particular budget?	❑	❑
Do you know how to remedy it?	❑	❑	To other ones?	❑	❑
Have you calculated the consequences of your actions?	❑	❑	Have you settled on a course of action to rectify it?	❑	❑
Does a volume variance exist?	❑	❑	Do you know what the results of this will be?	❑	❑
Do you recognise what it is doing to your budget, now and in the future?	❑	❑	Will you monitor this in the future?	❑	❑
To other budgets?	❑	❑			

Expenditure: Price Variance

For the majority of budget holders, significant variances in expenditure will be of equal if not greater concern than those relating to revenues. After all, most budgets within a company are mainly or exclusively expenditure based. The price of items or services bought under the headings of start-up, direct, indirect and/or capital expenditure may simply be higher or lower than indicated in the budget – those raw materials and component parts imported from overseas may go up in price more than anticipated. Possibly the cost of fuel for heat, light and power might fall unexpectedly because an alternative supplier is found. You should be concerned about offsetting the price variance with decreasing the volume of your variable purchases while maintaining your income levels.

Expenditure: Volume Variance

Often, the prices of goods and services purchased remain must the same as predicted but the quantities used are above or below expected levels. This type of variance usually occurs when a business is being set-up, is diversifying into new products and/or markets and budgets are consequently more subjective than on other occasions. As an example, when starting up a concern, accountants, solicitors, consultants and other professionals may be referred to more than was first planned. Occasionally, quantities used will be less than predicted, for example, labour input into the production of a new line might fall as new technological equipment is mastered and its use maximised. A volume variance is extremely important to watch. It can point to ineffeciency in the use of costly resources and can have a serious impact on your business.

Expenditure: Timing Variance

The timing of expenditure is not always considered as fully as it should be at sectional or departmental level, where the overall effect of incurring cost earlier or later than planned is rarely apparent to budget holders there. Expenditure may be paid out sooner than envisaged – perhaps the budget holder stresses the urgent need for updated machinery now in order to maintain productivity. Alternatively, it could be incurred later, perhaps because of the strain that payment will put on cash resources and other budgets' planned expenditure. A checklist for controlling your expenditure is given on p.84.

No Significant Variances

Some budgets unfold almost wholly as planned, recording only minor revenue an expenditure variances. It is tempting to assume that the holders of such budgets are extremely skilful, have been fortunate that internal and external circumstances have not conspired against them and are highly successful. The reality is more likely to be that they have been ultra-cautious, underestimating revenues so that these are always achieved or exceeded slightly whilst overestimating expenditure, with additional purchases being made as necessary near to the end of the period to justify the level of expenditure set, and to ensure it remains at least the same for next year. In this light, review performance with a realistic eye. Remember you are striving is achieve improvement and success for your business.

VARIANCE REPORT

The layout and contents of your various variance reports will depend on the following factors.

1. The nature and detail of your business.
2. The content of your original budgets.
3. The detail available from your financial reports.

The attached sample may be of use to you in designing your variance report.

CONTROLLING EXPENDITURE: AN ACTION CHECKLIST

It is sensible to adopt a measured, step by step approach to controlling expenditure. Being able to say 'yes' to the following questions indicates that you are tackling expenditure variances in an appropriate manner and are therefore most likely to succeed.

	Yes	No		Yes	No
Are purchase prices high or lower than expected?	❏	❏	Profits?	❏	❏
Have you identified the effects of this?	❏	❏	Cash flow?	❏	❏
On budgets?	❏	❏	Have you decided how to deal with this volume variance?	❏	❏
On profits?	❏	❏	Do you know what the results of this will be?	❏	❏
On cashflow?	❏	❏	Is expenditure paid for sooner or later than planned?	❏	❏
Do you know how to amend this price variance?	❏	❏	Have you appraised the roll-on effects of this?	❏	❏
Have you worked through the consequences of your actions?	❏	❏	Upon budgets?	❏	❏
			Profits?	❏	❏
Are the quantities purchased more or less than anticipated?	❏	❏	Cash flow?	❏	❏
Have you estimated the knock-on effects?	❏	❏	Have you spotted a remedy for this timing variance?	❏	❏
Regarding budgets?	❏	❏	Do you realise what the consequences of your actions might be?	❏	❏

REMEMBER

DO:

- Define your measurement and variance reporting system when you are first setting your budgets.

- Select the timing of how often you report your variances based on what your business needs are. In a retail organisation you would expect to monitor and report on sales revenues weekly or even daily, while a service provider who issues monthly invoices would select monthly reporting.

- Combine the reporting of variances with a system of investigation into the causes of the variances and a process of taking action.

- Consider selecting some key variances which are critical to your business instead of giving the same emphasis to variances on each line of your budget.

DO NOT:

- Ignore positive variances. A positive variance tells you that the budget requires adjustment or that a favourable opportunity has arisen that could be exploited for further advantage.

- Assume that the variances you select to be measured and controlled will not require adjustment or refocus even during the current budget period.

Chapter 6

Performance Measurement

This chapter will help you to:

- understand the concept of measuring all aspects of business performance not just those described by financial targets;

- understand the principles of selecting the operational performance measurements best suited to your business;

- operate both financial and non-financial performance measures.

Performance Measurement

Measuring performance against budget is the standard tool whereby management measures both business with performance and managerial performance, the latter often being linked to bonus payments.

Distinctions between effectiveness and efficiency are frequently very helpful in discussing performance measurement.

Effectiveness is the accomplishment of a desired objective.

Efficiency is an optimum relationship between input and output.

Killing a bluebottle, which is irritating the hell out of you, with a sledgehammer may be effective, but it is not efficient.

Performance may be both effective and efficient but either condition can occur without the other. For example, a company may set 20,000 units as a production objective but, because of a material shortage, only 15,000 units may be produced with 100 per cent efficiency. Performance would be efficient but not effective. In contrast 20,000 units may be provided on schedule with horrible waste of labour and materials. Performance would be effective but inefficient.

WORD TO THE WISE
When setting up any measurement system you should ensure you communicate both what you are doing and why you are doing it to the people whose personal or departmental performance you intend measuring.

In short two major questions about performance
are:

1. Is the manager effective?

2. Is the manager efficient?

- Question (1) often deals with attaining a revenue
  or volume target.
- Question (2) is an input/output question that is
  given a level of revenue or volume output. Did the
  manager control the inputs as he should have?

WHAT PERFORMANCE SHOULD YOU MEASURE AGAINST?

As in all forms of measurement the important thing
is to select which performance you are measuring
against.

1. Historical performance

You will be familiar with your historic business performance and what factors have changed to influence your expectations for current performance.
Allowing for the changes in markets, assets, cost
structures, etc. over time a comparison with historical performance is useful. However you must
recognise that judging performance in this way has
serious limitations which include:

(a) allowing for changing conditions is very often
    completed in an unscientific manner and unless
    the value or volume effect is actually completed
    it can be a deceptive way of assessing change;

(b) historical performance could be significantly
    poor and judging current measurement and may
    only perpetuate inefficiency or ineffectiveness;

(c) you are limiting your view of the business to

internal assessment when the reality is that success and survival depend on your relative performance to your competitors in the market.

Measurement of historic performance is useful but should ideally not be the only basis of measurement you use. This past is an indicator of where you are, not of where you might or should be.

2. Budgeted performance

Provided your budgeting system is working at least reasonably well, the process will allow the setting and agreement of appropriate targets for the measurements selected by you as relevant and useful and targets set should have taken account of historical conditions, planned changes and identifiable external factors.

The usefulness, in comparing your performance measurements against budgeted targets, is that what you establish as a measurable variance against that target can be used to asses what management decisions or actions are required in the short-term.

Measurement against budget should be done in the knowledge that your budget itself may need constant refinement.

3. External benchmarking

This is without doubt the most useful of all basis of performance measurements. The very fact of assessing performance against what is achievable in the 'great outdoors' of the competitive market is a highly important information tool that can focus your business to look for ways of improving and what issues or activities should be targeted for change.

If competitive survival is based on working more efficiently, cheaply and quickly, just imagine how powerful a tool comparing quality, cost, performance

with an industry standard is. The
budgetary process, where possible,
would include the setting of internal
targets based on such information.
On a continuous basis both actual
and budgeted performance should
be assessed against outside bench-
marks in order to keep updating
your performance assessment
against changes in the market
place.

The comparison you will need to
make between what is achieved,
past performance and budget will
give rise to questions such as:

> **WORD TO THE WISE**
> It would be worth-
> while considering
> linking your perfor-
> mance measure-
> ment to incentives
> for your staff and
> managers.
> Establish the use-
> fulness and practi-
> cality of the mea-
> sures before this is
> done so that you
> are not tied into
> making payments
> on impractical, irrel-
> evant or flawed
> measurements.

- The appropriateness of the sales
  unit pricing structure of the
  business.
- Have costs increased, for example due to a currency exchange fluctuation, which has not been
  reflected in the sales pricing?
- Would a variation in the sales price lead to a drop
  or increase in volumes that would add net gain or
  loss to the bottom line?
- Are there opportunities to negotiate purchaser
  price variation on the basis of volume?
- Is the gross margin for all products or services
  uniform or are there loss leaders or profit wind-
  falls affecting the average?
- Does the value of opening and closing stock
  reflect current purchase cost?

The difficulty with external benchmarking is, of
course, actually getting hold of the information you
require on the performance of the industry and
your competitors. Your sources of information will
include:

- published accounts;
- trade journals;
- consultants' reports;
- on the ground knowledge;
- market analysis;
- information available under freedom of information legislation.

KEY PERFORMANCE INDICATORS

Today there is a new approach to the identification and preparation of performance indices, which once again focuses on the control function, even though many of the performance measures are not now financial ones.

The starting point is the identification of the business drivers – those critical success factors which will differ according to the organisation being looked at. Once these have been defined and agreed (for the current period) the next stage is to define the *Key Performance Indicators*.

This process can be surprisingly difficult because the *Key Performance Indicators* will have to meet two objectives.

- They must be appropriate to the business in question.

- They must be comparable both internally and externally to enable the organisation to benchmark its results.

Figures are useless without action. The trick is knowing where to take action for the best effect, in other words to identify the levels for achieving success.

Too many businesses fall through not following the basic rules of control. You need to watch the classical business indicators!

- Cash flow.
- Inventory turnover.
- Debtor days.
- Interest/Profit.
- Gross margin.
- Added value.
- Disproportionate growth in overheads.

A sample of a monthly KPI report used in a production environment is outlined in Figure 6.1 on page 95.

FIGURE 6.1
KEY PERFORMANCE INDICATORS 1998

	1997	YTD 1998	BUDGET 1998
Headcount			
Inventory Turn			
Accounts Receivable DSO			
Productivity			
Total Assets £'000			
Cost of Sales			
Materials			
Labour			
Overheads			
Buyouts % of Sales			
S.G.&A. % of Sales (Total)			
Scrap Rate			
Fact Ind. Pay % of Sales			
Total Factory Payroll % of Sales			
Total Payroll of Sales			
Direct. Comp. per Hour			
Net Profit %			
Interest as % of Profit			
Overhead Rate YTD			
Purchase Price Variance			
Currency Impact			
(Gain/Loss of Exchange)			

FINANCIAL RATIOS

There are many ratios that are used to monitor performance. While the most common are listed and illustrated below it is worth stressing that you must select what is most appropriate to your business in order to achieve benefit from the measurement.

The most common ratios are:

- gross profit margin;
- net profit margin;
- expenditure;
- current ratio;
- acid test ratio;
- debtor day ratio;
- creditor day ratio;
- sales per employee;
- investment efficiency ratio.

For the purpose of illustration, I will use a very basic profit statement and balance sheet to demonstrate the calculation of the ratios.

A PROFIT AND LOSS ACCOUNT

	£	£
Sales:		158,000
Opening stock	20,000	
Purchases	100,000	
Direct labour	25,000	
Closing stock	15,000	
Cost of sales		130,000
Gross Profit		**28,000**
Overheads:		
Rent, rates, water	3,000	
Wages	8,000	
Transport	1,200	
Heat, light, power	1,300	
Printing, stationery	800	
Telephone	1,000	
Depreciation	600	
Professional fees	600	
Postage	500	
Insurance	400	
Miscellaneous	300	
Total		17,700
Net Profit		**10,300**

A BALANCE SHEET

	£	£
Fixed assets:		
Equipment	11,000	
Vehicle	800	
		11,800
Current assets:		
Stock	15,000	
Debtors	34,000	
Cash	500	
	49,500	
Current liabilities:		
Creditors	34,500	
Bank overdraft	13,000	
	47,500	
Net current assets		2,000
Net assets		**13,800**
Financed by:		
Accumulated reserves	3,500	
Profit	10,300	
		13,800

THE CALCULATION OF FINANCIAL RATIOS

Gross profit margin $= \dfrac{\text{Gross profit x 100}}{\text{Sales}}$

Net profit margin $= \dfrac{\text{Net profit x 100}}{\text{Sales}}$

Expenditure ratios $= \dfrac{\text{Expenditure x 100}}{\text{Sales}}$

Current ratio $= \dfrac{\text{Current assets}}{\text{Current Liabilities}}$

Acid test ratio $= \dfrac{\text{Debtors and cash}}{\text{Current liabilities}}$

Stock turnover ratio $= \dfrac{\text{Cost of sales}}{\text{Average stock}}$

Debtor days ratio $= \dfrac{\text{Debtors x 365}}{\text{Sales}}$

Creditor day ratio $= \dfrac{\text{Creditors x 365}}{\text{Purchases}}$

Sales per employee ratio $= \dfrac{\text{Sales}}{\text{Number of employees}}$

Profit per employee ratio $= \dfrac{\text{Profit}}{\text{Number of employees}}$

Investment efficiency ratio $= \dfrac{\text{Sales}}{\text{Fixed assets}}$

Gross Profit Margin

The **gross profit margin** ratio enables you to examine the relationship between sales and direct costs and shows how successfully the firm is buying, selling and trading – all of which are likely to determine if it is going to success (or fail) on a long-term basis.

The ratio is given below and is followed by an example relating to the accounts just shown. The resulting figure can be compared alongside the trade average, which is a useful yardstick for measuring the firms performance.

$$\frac{\text{Gross profit x 100}}{\text{Sales}}$$

$$\frac{\text{£28,000 x 100}}{\text{£158,000}} = 17.7\%$$

Net Profit Margin

The **net profit margin** expresses net profit as a percentage of sales and is important because it indicates whether the business is truly profitable after all of the costs have been met. If it is not (or is perhaps not doing as well as in previous years or as hoped) then attention needs to be turned upon expenditure and to reducing parts of it in some way.

$$\frac{\text{Net profit x 100}}{\text{Sales}}$$

$$\frac{\text{£10,300 x 100}}{\text{£158,000}} = 6.5\%$$

This really is the best method of assessing whether your financial objectives for the business have been achieved.

Expenditure Ratios

It can be helpful to take each area of **expenditure**, whether 'administration', 'finance', 'distribution' 'rent, rates, water', 'wages' or whatever, to view them as percentages of sales. This is especially useful for comparing year-on-year changes and identifying causes of any reduction in the net profit margin.

The examples reproduced below after the ratio are for 'rent, rates, water' and 'heat, light, power'.

$$\frac{\text{Expenditure} \times 100}{\text{Sales}}$$

$$\frac{\pounds 3,000 \times 100}{\pounds 158,000} = 1.9\%$$

$$\frac{\pounds 1,300 \times 100}{\pounds 158,000} = 0.8\%$$

Sales Per Employee Ratio

The **sales per employee ratio** measures the income produced by each member of the firm's workforce. It enables you to monitor progress from one year to the next and to make comparisons with other, similar businesses operating in the same trade or industry.

The profit and loss account and balance sheet used are from a firm that is run by an owner manager and seven employees.

Sales

Number of employees

£158,000
------------------   =   £19,750
8

Profit Per Employee Ratio

Alternatively, judgements can be made with regard to the **net profit generated on average by each employee** of the business. Again, it allows performances to be set alongside those of earlier years or in other, comparable businesses active in the same marketplace.

Profit

Number of employees

£10,300
------------------   =   £1,288

Current Ratio

The **current ratio** is a simple one, which shows if the business is solvent or not.

If all the short-term debts to the bank, suppliers and the like had to be paid up tomorrow, there must be (at least) sufficient funds to meet them and, hopefully, enough would be left over to keep trading. If not, thought must be given to somehow increasing assets and reducing liabilities.

$$\frac{\text{Current assets}}{\text{Current liabilities}}$$

$$\frac{£49,500}{£47,500} = £1.04 \text{ (of assets for every £1 of liabilities)}$$

Acid Test Ratio

Of course, if a firm had to settle all of its current liabilities immediately, it would be difficult to convert stocks into cash very quickly so it may be wiser to exclude these from the calculation.

The resulting **acid test ratio** when applied to the relevant figures from the accounts, may reveal that the financial position is not quite as secure as it first appeared and steps may need to be taken to remedy this.

An obvious suggestion would be to reduce stock levels as promptly as possible, with the 'extra' cash being retained in case of need.

$$\frac{\text{Debtors and cash}}{\text{Current liabilities}}$$

$$\frac{£34,500}{£47,500} = £0.73 \text{ (of assets for every £1 of liabilities)}$$

Stock Turnover Ratio

As a general rule, for most trades and industries, **stock** should be kept as low as possible and turned over quickly, thus freeing cash resources and making the most efficient use of funds.

Clearly, the rate of turnover will vary according to circumstances but can be compared with the trade or industry average for assessment purposes.

$$\frac{\text{Cost of sales}}{\text{Average stock}}$$

$$\text{Average stock} = \frac{\text{Opening stock} + \text{Closing stock}}{2}$$

$$\frac{£30,000}{£17,500} = 1.71 \text{ times per annum}$$

Alternatively, do not use the average stock in your calculatoin but instead do the calculation using the stock on defined dates and measure the change in the ratio from one period to another.

Debtor Days Ratio

The **debtor days** ratio highlights the number of days taken by customers to settle their bills.

Not surprisingly, debts to the firm need to be paid as promptly as possible in order that a satisfactory cash flow is maintained at all times – and should certainly be received before equivalent monies are paid over to creditors. The time taken can be appraised alongside previous year's figures and what is considered to be acceptable in the marketplace.

$$\frac{\text{Debtors x 365}}{\text{Sales}}$$

$$\frac{£34,000 \times 365}{£158,000} \quad = \quad 78 \text{ days to be paid}$$

If your credit terms are 30 days this is a poor performance.

Creditor Days Ratio

The accompanying **creditor days ratio** indicates how long it takes for the business to meet its debts. Careful attention needs to be given to the figure produced by this ratio – in theory, it should be longer than that of the debtor days ratio and, in terms of cash flow, as late as possible. However, thought must also be directed towards the benefits of paying earlier for prompt payments discounts and to sustaining a decent working relationship with suppliers. There is little point in paying very late if you'll never be able to obtain raw materials from that source again!

$$\frac{\text{Creditors} \times 365}{\text{Purchases}}$$

$$\frac{£34,500 \times 365}{£100,000} \quad = 125 \text{ days to pay}$$

It would be surprising if you suppliers were happy with this payment performance. They are most likely charging a higher price to you to compensate for your dismal payment performance.

Investment Efficiency Ratio

The investment efficiency ratio indicates how efficiently the firm is using its fixed assets in terms of the sales produced by each £1 of equipment, machinery and so on. In essence, it shows whether or not fixed assets are earning their keep.

$$\frac{\text{Sales}}{\text{Fixed assets}}$$

$$\frac{£158,000}{£11,800} = £13.30 \text{ per } £1.00$$

REMEMBER

DO:

- Select the performance you are measuring against carefully to ensure the relevance of the measure to your business goals.

- Consider new ways of judging performance that will motivate your staff to achieve their own and your business goals.

- Communicate both the achievement of goals and the problems in performance to your staff.

- Remember your original business plan objectives and consider what measurements you have in place to monitor how you are performing against these.

DO NOT:

- Forget that you need a customer focus in selecting your performance measurements.

Chapter 7

Budgeting: A Management Tool

This chapter will help you to:

- know how to extend the use of your budgeting system beyond the traditional view of the function of budgeting as a cost control mechanism;

- understand how budgeting can support both the information analysis and decision-making process that forms such a vital part of the management of your business;

- know how to use flexible budgets, cash forecasting and pricing models.

Budgeting: A Management Tool

WHAT DOES USING BUDGETING AS A MANAGEMENT TOOL MEAN TO YOU?

The day to day operation of any business is a complex and dynamic process where you as a manager or owner have to deal with a range of issues, opportunities and problems in order to make the best decisions for the business to prosper.

There are elements of the budgeting process that will assist you significantly in the daily decision making tasks. The simplest and most effective of these are:

- **cash forecasting**;

- **flexible budgeting**.

This chapter will show you the techniques of both and demonstrate their usefulness in managing your business effectively.

CASH FORECASTING

What is a Cash Budget?

Definition: A cash budget shows how cash will flow into and out of a business over a given period of time, usually corresponding to the budget period. A cash budget will differ from your trading budget in that it defines the timing pattern of how income and costs effect actual cash receipts and payments in and out of the business.

Forecasting cash flow is an intrinsic part of the budgeting process – particularly for smaller compa-

nies. It is not sufficient to know that you are operate profitably, but you must manage the assets and
activity of the business well enough to ensure that
there are sufficient cash reserves available, both to
keep trading and to fulfil the business plans for
development and growth.

The funds flow and working capital needs of your
business will not necessary stay in line with the
timing of your business profitability. An expanding
profitable business may easily run short of funds by
the short-term and can plan to accommodate this
by borrowing short-term funds. A declining business may generate surplus funds for which income
generating uses could be found.

One principal must be remembered when cash
planning:

*A profitable business will generate positive cash
flows over time, but a business that is losing money
will eventually run out of cash.*

WHEN SHOULD CASH BUDGETS BE PREPARED?

Cash budgets should be prepared whenever profit
and loss accounts and balance sheets are prepared.
The first draft of your cash budget should be made
when the implications of the overall budget objectives are being worked out. Drafts should be
amended at each stage as the budgeting proceeds.
When your agreed annual income and expenditure
budget is finalised you should also finalise the
annual cash budget.

This cash budget will provide you with an overall
assessment of the cash flow implications of the
budget plans for the year and a general picture of
what cash planning issues need to be addressed.

HOW TO PREPARE A CASH BUDGET

The income and expenditure budgets, which you
have been prepared using the techniques you have

learned from earlier chapters, will form the basis of your cash budget.

Each element of your sales and costs must be examined to assess what are the targeted and likely cash flow consequences of your plans. The timing of the cash flows will determine the basis of the cash budget. The structure of the preparation process is not unlike that of the income and expenditure budgets.

- Review current factors influencing the flow of cash.
- Set out the cash budget assumptions.
- Prepare the cash budget from the income and expenditure plans and the cash flow assumptions you have set.

Review of Current Business Conditions Influencing Cash Flow

Each element of both your income and costs will have a definite cash timing impact on the business. Take your income and expenditure budget and review the cash timing of each line item. Group together the income or cost headings that have the same cash timing to make the cash budget clear and uncluttered.

The review you will undertake should include the following.

- In a retail business, your sales income will generate cash for you in the same period as the sales take place.
- If you business gives credit terms to your customers review both the credit terms offered and the terms actually taken.
- The timing of issuing your invoices may be critical to when you receive in payment, e.g. you

WORD TO THE WISE

When considering how and when you might use flexible budgeting, you will need to keep a focus on how you use your budget as a motivational tool within the organisation. It is important that the original budget which you so carefully matched to your business objectives is used as a primary annual target.

may have to issue invoices as soon as delivery is made and not at the convenient end of the week or month because your customers' accounting system may exclude from their payment runs invoices received after certain processing dates.

- Consider that the payment practices of different customers may vary.
- The payment of salaries and wages is usually in the period when the work is done. Some businesses operate on a 'back week' payment system.
- The element of salaries and wages cost arising from employers' social insurance cost is due for payment in the month following the wages period.
- Certain overhead costs are incurred annually (e.g. insurance premiums, property rates, etc.) these should be shown on your cash budget as one composite group.
- Your business may pay a range of suppliers for goods and services according to different credit terms and it may be possible to agree standard terms with all suppliers to assist both the administration and planning of your cash flows.
- Examine how your stockholding policies and practices are affecting cash payments for your costs of goods sold. You may sell for the Christmas gift trade in November, but you could have held a stock of products for some time before the sale took place. The cash effect of the purchase you made of these goods could be months in advance of the sale taking place or the sales cash being received.
- Your company policy in availing of suppliers' discounts will impact on your cash outflow timing.
- Review the budget for items not included in the income and expenditure targets, e.g. the purchase or disposal of fixed assets.
- Include the cash flow inputs and outputs of financing deals or loan repayments.

Set Out the Cash Budget Assumptions

Having reviewed the current conditions which effect cash inflows and outflows you need to set the assumptions you will use in budgeting for cash in the future. These assumptions must include the effect of changes in trading conditions planned or targeted as a result of your review.

Your basic business cash flow assumptions should include:

- payment terms offered to customers;
- policy for implementing the agreed terms to customers;
- suppliers' payment terms;
- stock holding targets;
- timing of capital payments and receipts.

Use the Assumptions Developed to Prepare the Cash Budget Statement

The most effective way of ensuring completeness and accuracy of the cash budget is to use the budgeted profit and loss and balance sheet as your checklist for preparing the cash budget form.

The steps to filling in the budget form are as follows

1. Take each heading of income, cost, capital outflow and capital receipt and plot that into the cash budget form. Many headings, which have the same cash timing characteristics, can be grouped together for ease of presentation.
2. Group the cash inflows and outflows together from whatever source.
3. Show the totals for each.
4. Show the amount of net inflows or outflows.
5. Take you actual opening cash position and compute the closing cash position by adjusting for the net flows in the period.
6. The resulting closing balance will give you a bud-

get for your cash surplus or your financing requirements in the period under review.

Example of a Cash Budget

The following basic profit and loss budget statement can be used to prepare a cash budget for the period as an illustration of the techniques involved.
Insert here

Figure 7.1: Basic Example: Profit and Loss Statement

Profit Budget	January	Febuary	March	Total
Sales (a)	250000	400000	150000	800000
Less: Direct costs				
Cost of matersials	95000	150000	40000	285000
Wages	60000	90000	55000	205000
Gross profit (B)	95000	160000	55000	310000
Gross profit margin (A-B + 100%)	38%	40%	37%	39%
Overheads:				
Saleries	23000	23000	25000	71000
Rent, rates, water	10500	10500	10500	31500
Insurance	1000	1000	1000	3000
Repairs, renewals	1800	1200	1800	4800
Heat, light power.	600	600	600	1800
Postage	500	500	500	1500
Printing, Stationary	1000	1000	1000	3000
Distribution costs	1700	29000	15000	61000
Telephone	1100	1100	1100	3300
Professional fees	500	500	500	1500
Other	1200	1300	1400	3900
Total overheads (C)	58200	69700	58400	186300
Trading profit (B-C)	36800	90400	-3400	123700
Less depreciation	15000	15000	15000	45000
Net profit before tax	21800	75300	-18400	78700

The following are the cash flow assumptions used in the cash budget example given on page 118.

- The businesses had no sales or costs in the prior month of December.
- Receipts from sales are collected as follows:
  - 10 per cent of a month's total are cash sales;
  - 90 per cent of a month's sales are for credit;
  - credit period of 30 days.
- Stocks of direct materials are held for two months in advance of the sales period.
- Direct materials are paid for one month in arrears.
- Employers' social welfare costs are 10 per cent of the total wages and salaries bill.
- Wages and salaries in paid in the actual working month.
- Employers' social welfare costs are due a month in arrears.
- Rent and rates are due quarterly in advance. Water is paid monthly.
- Insurance premiums are paid annually. Credit of one month given by the insurance broker.
- Most overhead costs are due for payment when incurred.
- Distribution cost are payable weekly to the van rental company in the period the delivery takes place.
- Depreciation has no cash impact.
- Purchases of capital equipment and loan repayments are scheduled.

> **WORD TO THE WISE**
> When defining the assumptions that will form the basis of your cash budgeting you should place heavy emphasis on current practice and performance. While improvements in debt collection for example is a good performance target your cash forecast should be based on real conditions as the timing sensitive for cash management is critical.

Figure 7.2: Cash Budget

Cash Budget	January	Febuary	March	Total
Cash Inflows				
Sales Receipts	25000	265000	375000	665000
Sale of Lease			100000	100000
Total	2500	265000	475000	765000
Cash Outflows				
Cost of materials	15000	4000	80000	270000
Wages/Salaries	74700	101700	72000	248400
Social Insurance		8300	11300	19600
Rent, rates, water	30500	500	500	31500
Insurance		12000		12000
Repairs, renewals	1800	1200	1800	4800
Heat, light, power	600	600	600	1800
Postage	500	500	500	1500
Printing, stationary	1000	1000	1000	2500
Distribution costs	17000	29000	15000	61000
Telephone	1100	1100	1100	3300
Professional fees	0	0	0	0
Other	1000	1000	1000	1000
Operating Outflows	277700	197400	184800	659900
Capital Purchases	60000			60000
Loan repayments	0	45000	0	45000
Total	337700	242400	184800	764900
Net Inflows.outflows.	-312700	22600	290200	100
Opening Cash	200000	-112700	-90100	200000
Closing Cash	-12700	-90100	200100	200100

What does this Example Show you?

- The periods where you are making the best profit do not necessarily correspond to the best cash flow periods.
- All business events whether arising from normal trading or once-off capital events need to be included in the cash budget.
- It is prudent to set the assumptions more conservatively for the cash budget than you would for the profit budget.

The sales budget may contain some element of difficulty for your sales force to reach and the timing of the sales may be subject to risk. While you may like to set a target to collect your cash from debtors in 30 days but the current business experience is that half of the customers will take extended credit of 60 days. The cash budget should be realistically stated to reflect the most likely outcome not necessarily the targeted outcome.

- You may need to examine a number of cash flow outcomes in order to assess the impact of basis assumptions not being fulfilled, e.g. customer payment days terms not being achieved. This would be advisable in setting your short-term finance or overdraft requirements.

What is a Cash Forecast?

A cash budget is prepared as part of the budget process in your business, usually annually, and ties in with the formal target setting for the budget period.

A cash forecast is prepared on the same basis as the cash budget but is generally done for shorter periods and uses the actual trading figures for the most current period to predict and plan for short-term cash flows. In other words, it is concerned with the cash flow effects of actual activity rather than planned or targeted activity and thus it is a dynamic tool for managing your day to day operations. The purpose of a cash flow forecast is to show changes in cash asset requirements during the budget period so that immediate action can be taken to cope with short-term change and timing difficulties.

Example of a Cash Forecast

Take the example of the business budgets used above.

Report on the actual results from trading that were achieved by the business up to the end of February. Amend your cash budget and make it into a cash forecast by showing the cash flow effect of the actual results that have been achieved.

The following example demonstrates the use of a cash forecast as a very active management tool to control your cash requirements.

Figure 7.3: Cash Forecast

PROFIT BUDGET	JANUARY ACTUAL	FEBRUARY ACTUAL	MARCH FORECAST	APRIL FORECAST
CASH INFLOWS				
Sales receipts	15000	150000	175000	375000
Sale of lease			100000	100000
TOTAL	15000	150000	275000	475000
CASH OUTFLOWS				
Cost of materials	150000	40000	80000	80000
Wages/Salaries	74700	101700	72000	72000
Social insurance		8300	11300	11300
Rent, rates, water	30500	500	500	500
Insurance		12000		
Repairs, renewals	1800	1200	1800	1800
Heat, light, power	600	600	600	600
Postage	500	500	500	500
Printing, stationary	500	1000	1000	1000
Distribution costs	17000	29000	15000	15000
Telephone	1100	1100	1100	1100
Professional fees	0	0	0	0
Other	1000	1500	1000	1000
Operating outflows	277700	197400	184800	184800
Capital purchases	60000			
Loan repayments	0	45000	0	0
TOTAL	337700	242400	184800	184800
NET INFLOWS/ OUTFLOWS	-322700	-92400	90200	290200
OPENING CASH	200000	-122700	-215100	-124900
CLOSING CASH	-122700	-215100	-124900	165300

Period: MARCH /APRIL

In this example, the changes in circumstance that the actual trading results brought about were that:

- the value of sales achieved in January was £150,000 and the £250,000 originally budgeted;
- the timing of the February and March sales were reversed.

As the ordering of stock for direct materials has to be done three months in advance, it was not possible to defer the purchases of these materials in time to reduce requirements because of the drop in sales. As a consequence, the value of stock held at the end of February which was budgeted originally at £300,000 (March costs £150,000 plus April costs £150,000 not previously shown) is as was originally budgeted, and therefore the amount held is greater than the targeted level of two months requirements.

While the sales income inflows was the only major item to change from budget to actual, the cash flow difference between the budget and forecast is very significant. This demonstrates the importance of cash forecasting for your business management.

THE COST AND VALUE OF CASH

If funds are short, cash can be borrowed at a cost. If funds are in surplus even for as short a period as overnight, they can generate an income through interest.

Cash budgeting is a basic necessity for any business plan to be presented to a bank or lending institution for short or long-term financing. Your bank manager will be interested in both the validity of the assumptions used as well as the actual figures you have prepared.

Use your cash forecasts for best effect by treating

them as markers for issues to be addressed, for example:

- offer discounts to customers for early payment;
- cancel purchase orders early to react to changing stock levels;
- defer your capital equipment purchase to a later period if possible;
- extend the loan repayment period.

Cash Forecasting is both Necessary and Effective

Effective cash flow management requires efficient cash flow forecasting and effective cash flow management is a necessary part of you business survival.

Flexible Budgeting

A difficulty that many companies experience with the budgeting process is that it sets targets for a period during which there will inevitably be changes in both external and internal factors effecting your business. These may be either positive of negative changes to your prospects for profit and success. Managers and staff can get very frustrated when the performance reporting against the original budget during a budget period in which significant changes have taken place becomes less and less relevant to the actual day to day management of the business.

Budgeting can lose its effectiveness as a management tool unless some form of flexible budgeting and continuous forecasting is used throughout the budget period to take account of changing circumstances. By using flexible budgeting you can make your budget process a real part of managing your operations and an effective prompt for action.

Flexible budgets provide a basis for dealing with change in the budget period. The type of changes that would give rise to a need for a continuous fore-casting process would be:

- significant movement in currency rates affecting sales values which can not be absorbed in the budget period because of fixed price contracts;
- a change in the timing of sales or income invoic-ing. You may in this case stick to your overall sales target for the year but need to re-forecast the sales and cost spread over the remaining periods to the year end. When doing your month-ly variance analysis particularly by manager responsibility, it may be more appropriate to report the variances each month against the fore-cast and not the original budget spread;
- a deferral or a timing change of a new product launch;
- a decision on capital investment not originally taken into the expenditure budget for its impact on savings on maintenance costs or unit costs of production through improved efficiency;
- wage increases negotiated nationally which were not anticipated;
- costs not anticipated arising due to revised Health and Safety Regulations.

The continuous forecasting should be devised to off-set events during the year that, although uncertain in their affect or timing, would make the budgets unrealistic if these events occured.

Amending your budget in your flexible budgeting and forecasting process should be as well controlled and structured as your methodology for setting the budget in the first place. The process of control and approval is equally important when preparing fore-casts. It is sensible to keep monitoring your budget in conjunction with your forecast in the same care-ful and conscientious manner, studying and checking revenues and expenditure regularly, identifying and attending to variances promptly and drawing the management team's attention to problems, as and when appropriate.

The outcome of the review and forecasting process could generate actions such as:

- cost cutting to offset the effect of a down turn in sales volumes;
- bring forward introduction of new product to meet inadequate sale volumes;
- change pricing;
- defer capital expenditure.

The following is an example of a forecast form that you could consider adapting for your business needs.

Figure 7.4: Profit and Loss Forecast Statement

	MONTH			YEAR TO DATE			BAL OF YEAR	FULL YEAR	
	Actual	Budget	Variance vs Budget	Actual	Budget	Variance vs Budget	ESTIMATE	Estimate	Variance vs Budget
	1	2	3	4	5	6	6	7	9
SALES VOLUME									
SALES REVENUE									
LESS VAT									
SALES EXCLUDING VAT									
VARIABLE COSTS									
GROSS CONTRIBUTION									
OPERATING COSTS									
Manufacturing									
Engineering									
Distribution									
Marketing									
Sales Force									
Administration									
Total Operating Costs									
OPERATING PROFIT									
Other Income/(Costs)									
TRADING PROFITS									
Interest Income/(Cost)									
PROFIT BEFORE TAX									

The element of the budgeting process that is critical to your business success is the action you take to solve problems or grasp opportunities. These are identified in your review of performance against your budget targets. Flexible budgeting and forecasting are valuable tools in supporting you in this process.

REMEMBER

DO:

- Prepare cash forecasts for a shorter period than your master budget. It needs to reflect changing circumstances, particular issues of timing that will arise in any dynamic environment.

- Use the techniques and skills you have learned for your annual budgeting to support the process of examining the commercial and financial viability of new products, processes or markets.

DO NOT:

- Discount the possible advantages the use of flexible budgeting can give to your management of the business, despite the extra workload.

- Reduce the impact by too much detail when deciding the format for your cash budget and forecast. The critical element of cash control is timing so you will be likely to need only total expenditure and revenue headings.

Chapter 8

Capital Expenditure Budgets

This chapter will help you to:
- understand the nature of capital budgeting and why it is different to budgeting for income and expenditure;
- prepare capital budgets in a structured way in order to evaluate the business impact of your capital purchasing decisions;
- assess the strategic benefits to your business of good capital budgeting.

The Capital Budgeting Process

Capital expenditures are normally regarded as investments to acquire fixed or long-lived assets from which a stream of benefits is expected. The various techniques of capital appraisal can be applied to any expenditure which promises future benefits. Such expenditures delineate the firm's future operating capability and thus form the basis upon which the firm's future prosperity largely depends. Capital budgeting refers to the whole process of creating, appraising and implementing capital projects. Capital budgeting is concerned with more than using the 'correct' appraisal techniques or the correct completion of capital appropriation request forms.

The key stages in the capital budgeting process are set out below. The process outlined covers the formal steps typically required in most medium-sized organisations. Its primary aim is to ensure that the limited capital resources available to your business are allocated to wealth-creating capital projects that make the best contribution to your business goals.

A second goal should be to see that good investment ideas are not held back and that poor or ill-considered proposals are rejected or further refined.

WORD TO THE WISE
The basic difference between capital and revenue budgets is the definition of the timescale that you need to consider. Capital investment generates a stream of benefits over a relatively long period of time. These benefits must be evaluated against a reasonable measure of return in order to evaluate the appropriateness of the capital project.

Stage 1: Determination of the Budget

- How much is available to spend?

The fixing of what capital money is available to spend is sometimes a very difficult part of the process. As much capital funding is financed by borrowings, it is only when the appraisal of the project is being completed that you will determine what the capital needs or the borrowing capacity might be. Your starting point should be to determine what funds are available from existing resources, either cash assets or existing borrowing capacity.

Stage 2: The Search Process

- What project ideas have emerged?
- What costs and benefits will they generate?

Seeking-out ideas to exploit is arguably the most important part of capital budgeting, since without research and development and exploitation of new products and markets, firms are likely to wither and die. Over time, firms accumulate a 'stock' of project proposals (some of which may have been rejected previously) which are continually refined and re-examined as more information emerges. Evidence tends to suggest that the best *ideas* emerge from an unstructured research process but that the best *projects* emerge from a more highly controlled development process.

Stage 3: Evaluation

- What is the value of the projected costs and benefits?
- What is the target rate of return?

- Does the project's return exceed this?
- How risky is the project?

All relevant information about a project is exposed to the same format of evaluation or arithmetic analysis using one or several of the available techniques for computing project worth. At this stage, rigorous sensitivity analysis should be conducted to assess the uncertainties surrounding the project and the extent to which the project can underperform before it is no longer viable.

The preliminary project review conducted at this stage provides management with an early indication of the attractiveness of projects. Those not worth pursuing further are identified at an early stage, thus avoiding unnecessary managerial effort. Those worthy of further investigation are then given the 'go-ahead' to allow the sponsor to co-ordinate the many activities associated with producing a detailed appraisal request and to prepare for project implementation should approval be granted.

The capital evaluation form should provide the basis for a good evaluation so that the final decision to commit financial and other resources to the project can be made.

Typical information included in an evaluation form is:

- **purpose of the project**: why it is proposed and how it fits into the budget strategy of the business;
- **project classification**: e.g. expansion, replacement, modernisation, cost saving, quality improvement, research and development, safety and health, legal requirements, etc.;
- **finance requested**: amount and timing, including net working capital, etc.;

- **operating cash flows**: amount and timing, together with the main assumptions influencing the accuracy of the cash flow estimates;

- **attractiveness of the proposal**: expressed by standard appraisal indicators, such as net present value, DCF rate of return and payback period calculated on after-tax cash flows;

- **sensitivity of the appraisal indicators**: the effect of changes in the main investment consequences. Other approaches to assessing project risk should also be addressed, e.g. best/worst scenarios;

- **review of alternatives**: why they were rejected and their economic attractiveness;

- **implications of not accepting the proposal**: some projects which may have little economic merit according to the appraisal indicators may be 'essential' to the continuance of a profitable part of the business or to achieving agreed strategy.

Stage 4: Implementation and Monitoring

- During implementation, is the project on schedule?
- Will costs exceed the budget?
- Ongoing monitoring – is the project performing to budget? If not, why not?

Setting-up an investment project often becomes the province of engineers and production managers, but close financial and control and monitoring is required to minimise the extent of cost and time overruns, and to provide early warning signals of such difficulties. The term 'monitoring' is also applied to the observation of project performance, once it is 'up and running', i.e. producing outputs with definable costs and revenues. Most firms will incorporate the expected impact of a new project into their budgeting procedures, and can observe, very quickly, usually on a monthly basis, how well or badly the project is performing, and then take appropriate remedial action.

Stage 5: Post-auditing

* Is the project performing to initial expectations?
* How justified were those expectations?
* What lessons can we draw to assist future appraisals?

Once a project is established and early teething troubles have been ironed out, it is advisable, to examine in finer detail its success or otherwise in the light of initial expectation. There are many reasons for doing this, not least being the aim of testing the thoroughness of the original project evaluation in order to improve the quality of future appraisals. This should enhance the likelihood of acceptance of the 'best' projects, which should, in turn, enhance your business performance.

Post-auditing is a particularly important component of the capital budgeting system. If, as many executives contend, investment capital is a scarce or expensive

WORD TO THE WISE
The process of evaluating a completed capital project or investment or post-auditing, is vital to your success. Do not neglect this part of the process. It will give invaluable information not just about the success of the decision you made but also about the success of the evaluation process itself.

commodity, it is vital that maximum benefits are obtained from it, and that potential future errors of misallocation are minimised.

STRATEGIC IMPLICATIONS

Today, within most organisations, certainly larger ones, capital budgeting is viewed as part of a bigger process, the focus moving away from the project in isolation to the project within strategic business planning. A business strategy is a set of well co-ordinated action programmes aimed at securing a long-term sustainable advantage. As strategy frequently emerges through a process of backing those parts of the business viewed as 'winners' and eliminating 'losers', capital investments should be viewed within the strategic context. Capital expenditure proposals should be assessed in terms of their impact on longer term strategy to see if they fit into the overall framework in conjunction with the current activities of the business.

> **WORD TO THE WISE**
>
> In making your capital appraisal reflect careful on the risk elements inherent in a long-term evaluation. Use all the outside information you can to assess and measure he business risks so that they can be factored into the financial and business appraisal.

INVESTMENT ANALYSIS

Surveys of capital budgeting practices suggest that for many organisations, good investment decision-making is not necessarily synonymous with formalised capital budgeting procedures or the application of textbook appraisal techniques, at least in a strict sense.

The obvious danger is that, while we concentrate

on project appraisal methods, much of the rest of the capital budgeting process is largely ignored. At the outset, then, let us recognise a few 'home truths' about capital budgeting.

1. Theoretically correct methods may not, in practice, product optimal investment solutions.
2. Good investment projects do not simply emerge out of the woodwork – they have to be identified, defined and revised.
3. Project risk can rarely be measured in the manner prescribed in textbooks with any great level of accuracy.
4. Non-quantifiable aspects frequently have a significant impact on the decision outcome.
5. Estimates are rarely free from bias.
6. Managers, like politicians, frequently operate to hidden rather than explicit agendas.

In short, the application of formalised investment procedures and sophisticated investment techniques do not automatically deliver better quality investment decisions. We now turn to the application of capital budgeting in practice, where something of a revolution in adopting new methods has occurred in recent years.

Capital expenditure proposals are usually evaluated using one of or a combination of the three most popular methods:

• discounted cash flow;
• payback period;
• internal rate and return.

Discounted Cash Flow

The discounted cash flow model for capital decisions recognises that the use of money has a cost, (interest) just as the use of a building or car may have a cost (lease rent).

A pound in the hand today is worth more than a pound to be received or spent in five years' time. Because this evaluation method explicitly weights the value of money, it is the best method for use in evaluating long-term decisions.

Another factor in this method's favour is that it concentrates on cash inflows and outflows rather than on net profit in the accounting sense.

The difficulties in using this method are:
• setting the rate of discount to be used;
• it is a mathematical calculation, which is difficult to explain to non-financial managers.

Payback Period

Payback period is a rough and ready method that general textbooks try to ignore.

Yet it is the method most commonly used because it is easy to compute, understand and explain. Essentially payback period is a measure of the time it will take to recoup in the form of cash from operations only the amount of the original funds invested. Given the useful life of an asset and uniform cash flows, the less the payout period, the greater the profitability, or given the payback period, the greater the useful life of the asset, the greater the profitability.

The major weakness of this appraisal method is its neglect of profitability. The mere fact that a project has a satisfactory payback does not mean that it should be selected in preference to an alternative project with a longer payback time. In addition it does not consider the profile of the cash flows within the payback period itself.

Do not forget that the strong popularity of payback with managers is not entirely without justification. Its strength is that it is a simple measure of ranking projects where cash constraints prevail and it is a good first level screening device.

Many firms resort to payback when they have cash flow problems. It is seen as useful in times of high levels of uncertainty and high inflation as it assumes that risk is time related, i.e. that you will have more confidence in making estimates of forecasts for earlier periods.

Internal Rate of Return

This method uses a predetermined rate of return on investment and rejects or accepts proposals on the basis of meeting the target rate of return set. The difficulty is in setting the target in the first place and evaluating proposals which are seen as 'marginally' good or bad.

In real life a combination of the above methods tend to be widely used. The real difficulty in capital appraisal is in assessing future business risk and in long-term forecasting of cash, costs or revenues.

THE DECISION

It has to be admitted, however, that financial criteria may not be the only or even the main ones taken into consideration by management in making capital expenditure decisions. Strategic fit of an investment proposal is extremely important, even if financial returns are low.

Even in companies employing sophisticated systems of appraisal, capital projects tend to overspend, run late and under-earn. This can reflect the ego trip of the managers preparing proposals and/or internal competition for scarce funds. Statements like those below are not uncommon and must be guarded against.

- 'We will just have to find a way to get this project through.'

- 'Our competition is going to have one – we have to.'

- 'We must have one before our competitors.'

Most managers have limited skill in evaluating capital needs and proposals, as it in not something they do every day and the element of risk assessment or judgement is very high. Add the complexities of new technologies, the hard sell of salesmen and glossy new sales literature for the product and you can find that it is very difficult to make a reasoned assessment.

The main aim of this chapter is to emphasise that capital budgeting should be viewed as a multi-stage decision-process which should follow the pattern and methodology of all your budget preparation techniques.

MAKE OR BUY DECISIONS

The techniques to use when you are faced with business decisions, such as make or buy, can borrow a lot from the process outlined for capital budgeting.

The decision whether to make or buy depends on a number of factors.

1. Type of product

Product modifications and improvements are likely to follow the existing pattern, whether this is to make or to buy. A completely new original product is likely to require much more careful study to determine the procurement method.

2. Expertise and capacity

If the firm has the technical know-how and technical expertise, the preferred course is to make, and buying-in would only be considered if capacity is short or it the existing facilities are unsuitable for the new product.

3. Patents, licences and trade marks

There may be legal difficulties in deciding whether to make or buy at the first stage of product development. In particular, the business will register patents and trade marks as soon as possible and will be aware of the problems of infringing patents held by competitors.

It may be not possible to obtain a licence from another patent holder to manufacture, so the product must be bought in.

If the firm holds a patent, it must beware of losing control over it by indiscriminate licensing to subcontractors, in which case there is no alternative to self-manufacture.

Sometimes the original product innovator may own or have access to suitable production facilities. The firm then buys-in the product and assumes overall responsibility for marketing.

4. Timing

Timing is an important factor in make or buy decisions, since the business situation may change. The decision is a short-term one, which can be reviewed and changed.

- **Buy first, make later:** a product may be bought in at first and only manufactured if it is successful.
- **Make first, buy later:** the product may be manufactured from the start and the procurement subcontracted out only if the facilities cannot cope.

5. Cost aspects

- Straight cost comparisons between making or buying must be based on a careful analysis of the relevant costs, within the agreed timescale for the decision.
- For some firms the cost of making the product

is a small part of the total cost; the big expense of a product is telling the customer about it and providing the initial stocks to shops. For such firms the make or buy decision is not crucial – it is more important to make sure the product has distinctive features which will give a competitive advantage.

6. Risks

If the risk of product failure is high, purchase may be preferred, at least to begin with.

7. Global factors

In multinational firms, a formal appraisal of whether to make or buy and the location of manufacturing facilities/suppliers will be made on a worldwide basis as a matter of course, and all firms competing in their markets should approach their make or buy decisions in the same way.

REMEMBER

DO:

- Create an environment in your business that will help generate the ideas for capital investment for the future. In order to be able to assess possibilities for development, someone in your organisation is going to have to come up with the good ideas in the first place.
- Include all five stages of the capital decision making process in your work model for dealing with capital decisions. All stages are vital for success.

DO NOT:

- Forget that capital appraisal methods are necessary when you are considering the replacement of existing assets as well as the investment in something new.

Chapter 9

The Problems With Budgeting

By condsidering the problems and difficulties with budgeting this chapter will help you to:
- gain positive acceptance of the budget within the business and promote its use as a key to success;
- use the investment of time in the budget and monitoring process to the best effect;
- keep to a minimum the paperwork and administration workload in your organisation;
- stop the process demotivating you and your staff;
- achieve your budgeting and business goals.

The Problems With Budgeting

If budgeting is such a valuable tool in achieving financial success, why is it the case that organisations and business that adopt what appears to be a reasonable budget process, follow all the theoretical rules of preparation and monitoring, still have consistent difficulty in achieving their goals?

The reality is of course that businesses operate in a dynamic and uncertain environment where it can never be possible to plan and anticipate all the variables that affect the outcome of actions and events. In addition there are perceptions of the shortcomings and problems with budgeting that are very often true in the real world. It is worth considering these in order to find out what is the best view and style of budgeting management which suits your organisation. These are seen as the most common difficulties.

BUDGETING CAN BE INFLEXIBLE

Problem

I have often heard the statement made "we can not do that, it's not in the budget". Where such a philosophy is part of the way a business operates the budget process can be an impediment to success as it fails to adapt to changing circumstances and opportunities. It is fine as a method of controlling expenditure but when it is used as a way of stopping change or possible development it can lead to lost opportunities.

WORD TO THE WISE
To gain maximum benefit from your budgeting, you should continuously assess the value of the reports that your monitoring of the budget produces. What you need is value not volume.

Solution

The approach to overcome this is to use flexible budgeting as part of the budgeting process and philosophy of the company. Budgeting should never be used to restrict action but instead the process of planning and evaluation which it encompasses should be a support to the ever-changing needs of your business.

BUDGETING IS TIME CONSUMING

Problem

There is no doubt that this is a factor which affects the negative perception that can be held of budgeting. An enormous amount of time and effort is invested in some organisations in the budgeting process and in many instances it is viewed as being time, particularly management time, poorly spent. When you are starting and developing a budget programme there will also be additional time to be spent in the set up phase. But this is time worth investing in order that you get the maximum benefits from your budgets that have been detailed throughout.

Solution

The key to using the time that you have invested in budgeting successfully is to continuously examine and evaluate the success of the budgeting process and also its difficulties. Keep an open mind about what you retain or change in the process of budget setting, in order to limit the waste of time on issues or elements of cost or income that is of relatively little value.

Having a defined, structured approach in your goal setting, information gathering and the preparation of the budgets, as set out in the previous chapters, will help you to eliminate time-wasting and will increase your success.

BUDGETING INCREASES PAPERWORK AND ADMINISTRATION

Problem

Because you have decided to use budgeting as a way of developing and controlling your business, it is of course going to generate additional work and some would say even a life of its own. I have seen organisations produce significant and heavyweight budget manuals which never see the light of day once they have been prepared and approved.

Solution

The key to managing this problem is to continuously assess what information and reports are actually used and useful. This is particularly true of the variance reporting. The requirements will continuously change as problems are solved, costs controlled, projects completed and many valuable reports will no longer be necessary. It is up to you to decide what paperwork is generated. Remember you require value not volume. This may seem like a huge task, but it is only a reflection of what you should be doing anyway to manage your business for success. Be brave, consider the consequences of your actions, stay open to ideas and opportunities and your efforts will be rewarded by success.

BUDGETING DEMOTIVATES

Problem

The problem of budgeting being a demotivator primarily arise because budgeting serves a variety of purposes. Six key functions of budgets can be identified as:

- a motivational device;
- a means of forecasting and planning;
- a means of evaluation and control;

- a system of authorisation;
- a channel of communication and co-ordination;
- a source of information for decision-making.

The conflicts associated with these multiple functions of budgets cannot easily be resolved. In addition, budgeting operates in an environment where significant factors which influence the outcomes are not always controllable.

Solution

It is worth considering how budgets might be designed to achieve particular functions, how this leads to conflict and finally what lessons can be learned from practice.

In addition you need to recognise and respond to the behavioural issues that arise from using you budget as only a way of exercising cost control or restraint. If you use your budget in this way it will certainly demotivate. Keep the key functions always in mind in order to use the budget as a positive influence.

Now we can see three of the key functions identified above in more depth.

BUDGETING FOR MOTIVATION

There is a much evidence that supports the belief that budget targets have an impact on results, i.e. the budget is not just a neutral planning and controlling tool but in itself can help determine final outcomes. It is believed that 'tight but achievable' budgets normally lead to the best results, i.e. performance superior to that which would have been attained by other targets, or no targets at all. Thus if the budget is to be used as a motivational device leading to good results, then 'tight but attainable' budgets should be set.

Such budgets are, typically, of 'medium difficul-

The Problems With Budgeting   151

ty'. Consider the consequences if budgets are much tighter or slacker than this. It is highly possible that, if an easy budget is set, managers are likely to bring their aspirations into line with the budget-achieving less than if there had been no budget at all! Budgets cannot be used to motivate good performance if easy targets are set. Very difficult budgets are also usually associated with inferior performance, presumably because budget-holders perceive the budget to be unrealistic and are therefore not motivated by it.

This would seem to suggest is that the setting of very difficult budgets is highly risky and their possible negative impact on performance is dependant on how and when in the budget setting process, the budget holders own personnel goal or 'aspiration level' was set. The way in which budgets are prepared, i.e. whether imposed or via a participative process, can significantly affect how the balance between budget goals and personnel aspirational levels can be best achieved so that setting a difficult budget does not get a negative response and affect performances. It is wise to be extremely careful in setting difficult budgets and to be aware of the risk of demotivation.

BUDGETS FOR PLANNING

When 'stretching' budgets for individual departments, with significantly less than a 50 per cent chance of being achieved, are aggregated to produce a master budget, the master budget will have a very low probability of being achieved. It is acknowledged that stretch budgets are appropriate to motivate good performance. However, to organise a company around a plan with such a low chance of attainment is clearly inappropriate. An appropriate master budget for planning would be a realistic one, with the actual outcome being close to the budgeted outcome. However, if individual targets are reduced to make the aggregate budget more realistic then the motivational benefits of the individual budget will be lost.

It has been suggested that two budgets should be constructed – a realistic one for forecasting and planning and a more optimistic one for motivation. In practice this is rarely, if ever, done, possibly because the pain and misunderstanding that one budget can generate is sufficient for most organisations!

A possible solution to this may be to set budget holders personnel targets which are more challenging than the budget. However, the moti-

> **WORD TO THE WISE**
> Budgeting can fulfil a number of functions. Consider which ones are most important to you and build your budgeting style and reporting around the needs of your business.

vational impact of such targets will be crucially dependent on whether the budget holder can be persuaded that these goals, and not the budget, represent the 'real' target. This in turn will be dependant on the emphasis given to the attainment of each set of targets in the organisation's evaluation procedures and indeed in the payment of incentives.

BUDGETING FOR CONTROL AND EVALUATION

We have seen that the budgets of medium difficulty are associated with the best actual performance. Much evidence suggests that such stretching budgets produce excellent results, despite the fact that the results will, on average, fall short of the budget target. As this has implications for the way in which budget variances are used to evaluate the budget holder, placing him or her in a position of failure, then a number of behavioural consequences might be anticipated.

The manner in which accounting information is reported, and the consequences which follow from such reports, is an important determinant of the success of the budgeting process.

It is believed that in cases where there is a high level of environmental uncertainty, a fact of life for increasing numbers of businesses, a 'non-accounting' style appears to be most effective. With this style accounting data has only a small part to play in evaluating individual performance and budget adherence is not directly linked to rewards or punishment. An uncertain environment means that a manager's influence on actual outcomes is limited and the attempt to adhere rigidly to predetermined financial targets becomes inappropriate. If such adherence is required it is likely to lead to dysfunctional behaviour by the budget holder. Such behaviour ranges from the creation of excessive budgetary slack (requesting expensive budgets far beyond what is needed and being ultra conservative in setting revenue budgets) to falsification of accounting data.

On the other hand, if budget holders have both a high degree of control over budget outcomes and a high degree of independence, then heavy reliance on financial reports, termed a 'budget constrained style' does not appear to have negative consequences despite rewards and punishment being associated with budget adherence. This evidence suggests that care must be taken to adapt the reporting style to the circumstances of the budget holder if the most benefit is to be gained from budgeting.

THE BUDGETING PROCESS:
PARTICIPATION OR IMPOSED BUDGETS?
Problem
One of the difficulties of budgeting is the assessment of how much participation should take place throughout the organisation in the budget setting.

Not all organisations are the same and it is worth considering the level of participation most suitable to your needs.

Some evidence suggests that, with difficult budgets, performance is improved if individuals set their own aspiration levels after, rather than before, the budget is finalised. It might seem that participation in the budgeting process would ensure that minds remain open throughout the procedure, eventually giving budget holders 'ownership' of their budgets and leading to improved final results. However, while it may be politically correct to extol the virtues of participation, the hard evidence to support its value in the budgeting area are mixed. Many studies have shown the personality of the participants in the budgetary process is a significant influence on whether participation leads to improved performance.

Solution

Some evidence supports the view that some authoritarian people are unaffected by participative approaches while high participation is effective for individuals with a high need for independence and a low authoritarianism score. It may be possible to take this into account when deciding on the amount of participation that is appropriate for a particular budget holder, although this requires a high level of knowledge of the individuals involved.

Common sense and experience would suggest that the level of participation should relate to the level of job difficulty, participation is effective when the job difficulty and participation are high but that high participation is ineffective when job difficulty is low.

When a job is easy, an imposed budget may be readily accepted, but this is highly unlikely to be the case in a difficult and uncertain environment. This suggests that the level of participation required to get most from budgeting should be adjusted to the circumstances of the budget holder's environment, which would be easier to determine than the budget holder's psychological profile.

PRACTICAL OBSERVATIONS THAT WILL BE USEFUL TO YOU

A consideration of both budgeting theory and experience of budgeting practice would lead to two observations, which may be of interest to you in the budgeting process.

Consider your Objectives

First, I suggest that managers should give careful thought to the particular objectives that they are trying to achieve in budgeting. As it is difficult to achieve all the objectives of budgeting simultaneously, care must be taken to ensure that the process achieves the objective deemed to be most important. For example, if the company is in real difficulties, the most important business objective would be survival and the paramount budget objective would be to set a realistic plan to see the company through the coming year.

An imposed, cost-cutting budget might achieve this overriding objective. However, the target set should not be so harsh as to be viewed as impossible or the budget may actually make matters worse.

On the other hand, an expanding company may want to ensure that managers are motivated to grasp opportunities while they are available. Such a company might emphasise the communication, co-ordination and motivational aspects of budgeting while downplaying the planning, authorising and evaluative aspects.

Take Action to Minimise the Problems

A second observation is that, once managers are aware of the potential difficulties of budgeting they can take action to minimise the impact of the difficulties. For example, the alternatives of 'top down' and 'bottom up' budgeting are often set out as mutually exclusive alternatives. 'Top down' may be affective in forecasting and planning but, is likely to be ineffective as a motivational device in many circumstances. 'Bottom up', on the other hand, might aid communication and co-ordination but at the expense of control.

However, it is possible to involve budget holders in the development of their budget while still setting out fairly closely defined limits within which they are expected to operate. This avoids the 'wish list' syndrome where managers initially produce a set of budget requests which is greatly in excess of anything they expect to receive, because they expect to be cut back in subsequent rounds of budget negotiation.

To Get the Best Results

The best results in budgeting will be achieved when a complex mix of factors is taken into account:

• the personalities of the participants:
• the type of budget being set – expense or revenue-
• the degree of uncertainty present;
• the approach to performance reporting.

To incorporate all these factors successfully, requires a high level of sensitivity and excellent communication skills.

Getting the most from budgeting will always require both sound technical knowledge and sensitivity to the likely behavioural consequences of budgeting.

A careful analysis of what needs to be achieved and how the budget process can help, together with some common sense attention to the details of budgeting can make the process more useful and less painful.

REMEMBER

DO:

- Be flexible in your approach to budgeting and make changes as you need to.
- Select the budget style most appropriate to your business.
- Decide which of the functions of budgeting suits the needs of your business best.

DO NOT:

- Ignore the behavioural consequences of the budget style you adopt.
- Allow the possible problems to defeat your goal. There are solutions to be found if you examine, evaluate and take action.